THINKING
Skills for Success

THINKING
Skills for Success

Dr. Edward de Bono
Director, The Cognitive Research Trust

PARADIGM

Editor: Barbara G. Cox, Ph.D.
Editorial Consultant: Christine Maxwell
Writing Services: Jon H. Hoelscher
Design and Composition: Morris Lundin

Library of Congress Cataloging-in-Publication Data

De Bono, Edward, 1933-
    Thinking skills for success / Edward de Bono
       p.   cm.
    ISBN 1-56118-048-3
    1. Thought and thinking—Problems, exercises, etc. 2. Creative
thinking—Problems, exercises, etc. 3. Problem solving—Problems,
exercises, etc. 4. Success—Psychological aspects—Problems,
exercises, etc. I. Title.
BF441.D386 1990
155.4'2'076—dc20   90-7358
                                                    CIP

Printed in the United States of America.

10 9 8 7 6 5 4 3 2 1

Contents

PART ONE: BREADTH

UNIT 1

UNIT 2

UNIT 3

PART TWO: INTERACTION

PART THREE: INFORMATION

UNIT 1

UNIT 2

Introduction

About Thinking Skills

It may, at first, seem unusual to consider thinking a skill that should be explicitly taught. After all, everyone thinks. True, everyone possesses a natural thinking capability. There are also, however, thinking skills that can be learned and developed through practice. These skills are addressed in the series of lessons that compose this book.

First, let's clear up some possibly mistaken ideas about thinking. High intelligence is not the same as thinking. Many people with high IQs do not direct their thinking effectively. Knowing information does not necessarily mean that good thinking is taking place. Memorizing or acquiring facts is not the same as being able to use those facts as part of thinking skills. Also, thinking is not discussion, knowledge, intuition, having a point of view, or being able to express oneself well.

What, then, **are** thinking skills? They are practical and usable tools for applying the information and experience that a person already has and for gaining new understanding. This book presents thirteen proven tools and provides practice using these tools in situations, problems, or applications relating to general business. The purpose of developing thinking as a deliberate skill is to enable you to apply this skill to new and unfamiliar situations and problems that occur in daily living.

This approach to learning and developing thinking skills is proven, practical, and enjoyable. Everyone who uses this book can be successful at learning to apply a useful set of thinking tools to a wide range of situations, questions, and issues.

This publication is based in part on *The CoRT Thinking Program*, 2nd Edition, by Edward de Bono.* (CoRT stands for Cognitive Research Trust.) CoRT thinking lessons have been used since 1970 and are now used in thousands of schools internationally. They are effective with learners of all ages, abilities, and cultures.

Expectations

What can you expect from your study of thinking skills? The expectations work two ways. You will be expected to participate in and contribute to the discussions and to practice using the thinking skills you learn. In return, you can expect to be successful at developing thinking skills to better use your knowledge and experience as you continue to deal with an increasingly complex world. Specifically,

1. You will be asked to think about particular issues or situations.
2. You will learn to avoid immediately labelling questions or ideas "stupid" or "ridiculous," and to examine ideas from different perspectives before coming to a decision.
3. You will gain the confidence to think constructively about any idea, even if it seems different or remote.

---

*©1986, MICA Management Resources UK, Inc., and reprinted with permission of the publisher, SRA, a division of the Macmillan/McGraw-Hill School Publishing Company. The original sixty CoRT thinking lessons may be obtained from SRA.

4. You will learn to listen actively to the opinions of others. You will find yourself more willing to listen to the views of others rather than trying to prove your own view correct.

5. You will learn to look at situations more broadly and to consider more aspects of a situation.

6. You will learn to use thinking skills appropriately and will use them naturally as a routine part of your decision making.

These expectations will be met gradually, through the course of your participation and practice. As you learn, practice, and develop your thinking skills, you will become more confident applying the skills to different situations. Similar to a master craftsman who has practiced and developed his skills, you will be better able to understand a question or situation and deal with it by applying appropriate thinking tools.

Using This Book

Each lesson in this book aims to stimulate your thinking. The resources needed for this course are already present in your mind. You will not need to watch filmstrips or read textbooks to begin to think more effectively.

The lessons focus on specific thinking tools and provide practical ways to identify, learn, and use them. After every four lessons, a review lesson reinforces the skills you have learned. Thinking tools are developed in three areas: Breadth (Lessons 1 to 15); Interaction (Lessons 16 to 20); and Information (Lessons 21 to 30).

1. *Breadth.* The specific purpose of these lessons is to broaden your perception beyond the obvious, immediate, and personal.

2. *Interaction.* These skills concern thinking situations involving other people. They apply to arguments, debates, and negotiations, helping a thinker recognize and understand what is occurring in an interaction.

3. *Information.* These lessons are concerned with eliciting and assessing information. In business situations, rarely is more than thirty per cent of the required information available, yet decisions must be made. Applying good thinking can compensate for inadequate information.

You will participate in three types of activity while learning these thinking skills: large group discussion, small group discussion, and independent work. What is important is your repeated use of the tools, not the specific problems or situations you discuss.

1. Large group discussion involves the entire class. This level of discussion is used to introduce each of the thinking skills. First, each skill will be explained; you will learn how it works and how to use it. Then examples of using the skill will be discussed by the class.

2. Small group discussions will typically be in groups of four to five students. Small groups allow you to practice the skills with more discussion, disagreement, and give-and-take than large groups. Each group will apply the new thinking skill to specific problems or situations. Discussion must be fast-paced and focused; each item is allotted four to six minutes. It may prove helpful to have one person record the group's ideas. Then each group will share its ideas with the whole class in a follow-up large group discussion.

3. Individual work is written in response to specific problems or thinking situations. Such work allows further practice and individual application of the tools. There is space provided in this book for writing responses to the problems. If you need additional space, of course, use separate sheets of paper. Your instructor may suggest other problems or assignments during the course.

At first, the skills will be applied to general problems or situations. Then they will be applied to situations relating to the workplace or to personal decisions relating to your job. Many of the topics may be personally interesting. Remember, however, that the emphasis of the lesson is not on the topic, but on the thinking process or skill used to examine the topic. Focusing on the thinking skill will enable you to apply that skill to other topics and problems you encounter.

Part One

BREADTH

Skills that improve the breadth of your thinking.
Skills that broaden your perceptions.

UNIT 1

PMI: Plus, Minus, Interesting (Lessons 1 and 2)
CAF: Consider All Factors (Lessons 3 and 4)

PMI: PLUS, MINUS, INTERESTING

P = Plus   The good things about an idea; why you like it
M = Minus   The bad things about an idea; why you don't like it
I = Interesting   The things you find interesting about an idea

Instead of just saying that you like an idea, or don't like it, you can use a **PMI**. When you use a **PMI** you give the good points first, then the bad points, and then points that are neither good nor bad, but are interesting. You can use a **PMI** as a way of treating ideas, suggestions, and proposals. You can ask someone else to do a **PMI** on an idea or you may be asked to do one yourself.

EXAMPLE: DOING A PMI

Idea: All the seats should be taken out of buses.

P: More people can get into each bus.
It would be easier to get in and out.
Buses would be cheaper to make and to repair.

M: Passengers would fall over if the bus stopped suddenly.
Older people and disabled people would not be able to use buses.
It would be difficult to carry shopping bags or babies.

I: Maybe there should be two types of buses, one with and one without seats.
The same bus would do more work.
Comfort may not be so important in a bus.

PMI PRACTICE: SMALL GROUP ACTIVITIES

In small groups, do a **PMI** on the following ideas. Refer to the example in this lesson.

1. By law all cars should be painted bright yellow.

2. People should wear badges showing whether they are in a good mood or bad mood that day.

3. All students should spend three months every year earning money.

4. Every adult should spend one week a year in the police force.

5. There should be a special TV channel for young people only.

DISCUSS THE **PMI** PROCESS

1. When is a **PMI** most useful?

2. Does one always look at the good and bad points of an idea?

3. Does a **PMI** waste time?

4. Is it easy to do a **PMI**?

DISCUSS **PMI** PRINCIPLES

1. The **PMI** is important because without it you may reject a valuable idea that seems bad at first sight. Discuss.

2. Without a **PMI** you are very unlikely to see the disadvantages of an idea that you like very much. Explain.

3. The **PMI** can show that ideas are not just good or bad but can also be interesting if they lead to other ideas. Why is this so?

4. Without a **PMI,** most judgments are based not on the value of the idea itself but on emotions at that time. Explain.

5. With a **PMI** you decide whether or not you like the idea after you have explored it instead of before. How is this beneficial?

PMI PROJECT 1

Select one of the following items. Do a **PMI** on the idea. Use the space provided to record your responses.

1. All cars should be banned from city centers so that people can walk about freely.

2. Every young person should adopt an old person to care for.

P: _____

_____

_____

_____

_____

M: _____

_____

_____

_____

_____

I: _____

_____

_____

_____

_____

_____

_____

PMI PROJECT 2

Do a **PMI** on one of the following ideas. Use the space provided to record your responses.

1. People should be allowed to work ten hours a day for four days and have the rest of the week free, instead of working eight hours a day for five days.

2. In many countries there is a jury system in which ordinary people assess whether an accused person is guilty or not. Some other countries do not have juries but have three judges who do all the assessment themselves. Do a **PMI** on this three-judge system.

P: _____

_____

_____

_____

_____

_____

M: _____

_____

_____

_____

_____

_____

I: _____

_____

_____

_____

_____

_____

Lesson 2

PMI IN GENERAL BUSINESS

PMI PRACTICE: SMALL GROUP ACTIVITIES

Use your **PMI** skills to evaluate the ideas of the people involved in the following situations:

1. Lynn has been in a clerical job in the purchasing department and has accepted an advancement that will include buying office supplies.

    Idea: Impress the boss by reducing the cost of all items purchased.

2. Fred is a long-time employee who worked his way up from laborer to skilled machine operator. Due to personal problems, for the last six months Fred has been late and absent often and his work performance is way off.

    Idea: It is time to fire Fred.

3. Steve and Jane both work. Their son is sick and needs to be taken to the doctor. Jane cannot afford to take time off from her job.

    Idea: Steve will tell his boss that he is sick himself, so he can have time off and take their son to the doctor.

4. Valerie opened her florist shop two months ago. She is finding that about seven percent of the personal checks written by customers for the purchase of flowers are not good.

    Idea: Accept only cash or credit cards for payment.

USING **PMI** IN GENERAL BUSINESS

Use the space provided to record your responses.

1. When is it useful to do a **PMI**?

_____

_____

_____

_____

_____

2. What might happen if you do not do a **PMI** on an idea you like?

_____

_____

_____

_____

3. Why is it important to think of interesting aspects of an idea, not just plus and minus aspects?

_____

_____

_____

_____

_____

PMI PROJECT 1

Select one of the following items. Do a **PMI** on the idea associated with the situation.

1. The word processing group seems to be continually disrupted by the need to produce "rush" memos for managers and supervisors.

    Idea: All managers and supervisors have access to computer terminals or typewriters; they should produce their own memos.

2. In the machine shop, all machinists are required to keep their work area clean and swept throughout the day.

    Idea: Hire someone as a sweeper to keep the shop clean.

3. The home construction industry has been badly hurt by a long season of heavy rains that stopped outdoor work.

    Idea: Place an inflatable, reusable plastic dome over each work site until the outside of the home is complete, then move it to the next site.

P: _____

_____

_____

_____

M: _____

_____

_____

_____

I: _____

_____

_____

_____

_____

PMI PROJECT 2

Select one of the following items. Do a **PMI** on the idea associated with the situation.

1. A manufacturer has a long production line where each worker performs a small task as a product moves past his or her workstation. Boredom, injuries, and turnover are high.

    Idea: Form production teams that will stay in a work area and build the complete product from start to finish; the needed parts would be brought to their work area.

2   A delivery company finds that the drivers seem to be making fewer pickups and deliveries each day.

    Idea: Put a transmitter in each truck; then the trucks can be tracked by satellite and the supervisors can monitor the whereabouts of every truck at all times.

P: _____

_____

_____

_____

_____

M: _____

_____

_____

_____

I: _____

_____

_____

_____

CAF: CONSIDER ALL FACTORS

CAF = Consider All Factors

When you have to choose, make a decision, or just think about something, there are always many factors to consider. If you leave out some of these factors, your choice may seem right at the time but later will turn out to be wrong. When you are looking at other people's thinking, try to see what factors they have left out.

For example, some years ago in a big city there was a law that all new buildings had to have large parking lots in the basement so that the people working in the building would have somewhere to park. After a while this law was changed because it was found to be a mistake. Why? The city's lawmakers had forgotten to consider the factor of quantity: how many people would drive their cars to work? Providing parking lots encouraged *everyone* to drive to work and traffic congestion became worse than ever.

EXAMPLE: DOING A CAF

A husband and wife want to buy a used car for their family. They consider all the following factors:

1. That the person selling the car actually owns it
2. Price of the car
3. Type of car and the color
4. Engine power and speed of the car
5. Condition of the mechanical parts
6. Size

Can you think of any others?

CAF PRACTICE: SMALL GROUP ACTIVITIES

In small groups, do a **CAF** on each of the following items. Refer to the example in this lesson.

1. What are the factors involved in choosing a career?

2. An inventor has invented a breakfast pill; it's very tiny but contains all the food and vitamins you need. After you have eaten the pill you do not feel hungry for five hours. Should this pill be allowed? What are the factors involved?

3. What are the factors involved in choosing your hairstyle?

4. If you were interviewing someone to be a teacher, what factors would you consider?

5. The textile workers in a country demand protection from foreign imports that are coming into the country at a lower price and taking over the market. What factors should a government consider in the matter?

DISCUSS THE **CAF** PROCESS

1. Is it easy to leave out important factors?

2. When is it most important to consider all factors?

3. What is the difference between **PMI** and **CAF**?

4. What happens when other people leave out certain factors?

5. Do you need to consider all factors or only the most important ones?

DISCUSS **CAF** PRINCIPLES

1. Doing a **CAF** is useful before choosing, deciding, or planning. Why?

2. It is better to consider all the factors first and then pick out the ones that matter most. Explain.

3. You may have to ask someone else to tell you whether you have left out some important factors. Why is this a good idea?

4. If you have left out an important factor, your answer may seem right but will later turn out to be wrong. How can this be?

5. If you do a **CAF** on someone else's thinking, you may be able to tell the person what has been

CAF PROJECT 1

Select one of the following questions. List the factors that should be considered.

1. What factors should you consider in choosing a place to live?

2. A young couple is undecided about whether to get married at once or wait. What factors should they be considering?

Factors: _____

_____

_____

_____

_____

_____

_____

_____

_____

_____

_____

_____

_____

_____

_____

CAF PROJECT 2

Select one of the following questions. List the factors that should be considered.

1. What factors should you consider in designing a chair?

2. In deciding how to spend your vacation, what factors should you consider?

Factors: _____

_____

_____

_____

_____

_____

_____

_____

_____

_____

_____

_____

_____

_____

_____

Lesson 4

<u>CAF</u> IN GENERAL BUSINESS

CAF PRACTICE: SMALL GROUP ACTIVITIES

Use small group procedures to do a **CAF** on each of the following items.

1. What factors should be considered in hiring a secretary?

2. A company that manufactures hobby kits and toys wants to add a new product to its list. What factors should the company consider?

3. You want to open a chocolate shop. What factors should be considered in deciding where this shop should be located?

4. What factors should be considered in choosing the location of a factory to recycle used glass and metals?

5. In thirty days, a company will receive a very large payment for a job it just completed for its best customer. Unfortunately, the company is not sure it will have enough money coming in from other customers to pay all its employees and bills that are due before the receipt of that large payment. What factors must it consider in trying to solve this problem?

USING CAF IN GENERAL BUSINESS

Use the space provided to record your responses.

1. When is it useful to do a **CAF**?

_____

_____

_____

_____

2. What might happen if you do not consider an important factor?

_____

_____

_____

_____

3. Why is it useful to work with another person when doing a **CAF**?

_____

_____

_____

_____

4. How might it be helpful to do a **CAF** on the thinking of a customer of your company?

_____

_____

_____

_____

CAF PROJECT 1

Select one of the following items. List the factors that should be considered.

1. Your company has sales representatives all over the United States. What factors should be considered when planning the time and location of the annual company sales meeting?

2. A plan is under way to turn a golf course on the edge of a growing town into a new shopping center. The plan is backed by businesses and consumers but opposed by environmentalists. What factors should be considered in the final decision?

Factors:_____

_____

_____

_____

_____

_____

_____

_____

_____

_____

_____

_____

_____

_____

CAF PROJECT 2

Select one of the following items. List the factors that should be considered.

1. While you are working, you learn that one of your coworkers is stealing from the cash register. You wonder whether you should tell the supervisor in person or just write an anonymous note. What factors should you consider in making this decision?

2. Your company has retail stores all over the United States. What factors should be considered when planning the location of three new warehouses that will be used to receive large quantities of merchandise from manufacturers, store the goods, then send small quantities of the merchandise to the stores as needed?

Factors: _____

_____

_____

_____

_____

_____

_____

_____

_____

_____

_____

_____

_____

_____

Lesson 5

RULES

The main purpose of this review lesson is to practice **PMI** and **CAF**. Evaluating an existing or proposed rule requires use of **PMI**. Deciding what factors should be considered in making a rule calls for **CAF**.

ABOUT RULES

1. Some rules are made to prevent confusion, for example, the rule that cars must drive on one side of the road.

2. Some rules are made to be enjoyed, for example, the rules of football make the game of football.

3. Some rules are made by organizations for their own members, for example, the rule that soldiers must wear uniforms when on duty.

4. Some rules are made to prevent a few people from taking advantage of everyone else, for example, the rule that you must not steal.

5. In general, the purpose of a rule is to make life easier and better for the majority of people.

EXAMPLE

In most countries, cars are driven on the right side of the road. In Britain, however, they are driven on the left side. There is a suggestion that Britain should change from the left side to the right side to be like other countries. Before deciding to propose or make a rule, identify the factors involved.

Do a **CAF** on this situation.

Factors: Time and cost to change traffic signs around
            Re-education of drivers
            Placement of bus stops
            Placement of driver equipment in cars

Now that the factors are identified, do a **PMI** on the proposal that Britain change its law and require that cars be driven on the right side of the road.

P: Britain would be like other countries.

        Car manufacturers would only have to make one kind of seating arrangement.

        Foreign cars (with driver seat on the left) might have increased sales.

        People would buy new cars and that might be good for the economy.

M: Drivers might forget and drive on the wrong side, causing accidents.

        Changing traffic signs would be costly and take a lot of time.

I: What would happen to old cars?

RULES PRACTICE: SMALL GROUP ACTIVITIES

Follow small group procedures for each of the following items.

1. A group of people sail away to an island to start a new life. They abolish money, property, and all the old rules. Soon they find that no one wants to do the hard work needed to grow food and build houses. Do a **CAF** on the situation and then invent some rules that would help solve their problems.

2. A new rule has been suggested for employment. Instead of accepting a job for an indefinite period of time, the employees can sign a contract for one, two, or five years as they wish. At the end of the period, the employee and the employer would decide whether or not to enter another contract. Do a **PMI** on this idea.

3. Concerns have been expressed that young people buy and watch video tapes that are full of violence and are not suitable for them.

    a. What are the factors involved? Do a **CAF**.

    b. What rules could you devise to protect against this happening?

    c. Evaluate your rules by doing a **PMI** on them.

4. In a sailboat race there are all sorts of boats. Some are big and fast. Some are small and slower. You want everyone to have a chance of winning.

    a. What are the factors involved? Do a **CAF**.

    b. What rules could you set up?

    c. Evaluate your rules by doing a **PMI** on them.

DISCUSS THE RULES PROCESS

1. Which rules are good and which are bad?

2. Who makes rules?

3. What are rules for?

4. When are rules useful?

5. What is the difference between **PMI** and **CAF**?

DISCUSS RULES PRINCIPLES

1. A rule should be widely known and understood and also possible to obey. Why?

2. A rule is not a bad rule just because some people do not like it. Why not?

3. A rule should work for the benefit of most of those who have to obey it. Why?

4. Those who have to obey a rule should be able to see its purpose. Why?

5. From time to time rules should be examined to see if they still make sense. Why?

RULES PROJECTS

Use the space provided to record your responses.

1. If you were running an office, on which rules would you insist?

_____

_____

_____

_____

_____

2. Your company has twenty salespeople in the United States. The number of customers in each sales territory is not equal; some territories have only 100 customers; some have as many as 500. What factors should be considered in planning a sales contest? Do a **CAF** to list them. What rules would you make up for the annual sales competition so that each salesperson has a chance to win?

Factors:_____

_____

_____

_____

_____

_____

Rules: _____

_____

_____

_____

_____

_____

3. Many people are bothered by telephone sales calls. They feel the calls are an invasion of their privacy. Do a **PMI** on a proposal to outlaw telephone sales.

P:_____

_____

_____

_____

_____

_____

M:_____

_____

_____

_____

_____

_____

_____

I:_____

_____

_____

_____

_____

_____

_____

Select one of the following projects. Record your responses in the spaces provided.

4. In metropolitan areas traffic congestion is a problem between 6:30 a.m. and 8:30 a.m. What rules can you think of to solve the problem? Start by doing a **CAF**. Next invent your rules. Then do a **PMI** on two of your rules.

5. A company is having trouble because too many employees are coming to work late. What factors should be considered in trying to solve this problem? What rules would you make to solve it? Do a **PMI** on two of the rules you propose.

Factors:_____

_____

_____

Rules:_____

_____

_____

Rule 1, **P**:_____

_____

_____

Rule 1, **M**:_____

_____

_____

Rule 1, **I**:_____

_____

_____

Rule 2, P: _____

_____

_____

_____

_____

Rule 2, M: _____

_____

_____

_____

_____

Rule 2, I: _____

_____

_____

_____

_____

BREADTH

UNIT 2

C & S: Consequences and Sequel (Lessons 6 and 7)

AGO: Aims, Goals, Objectives (Lessons 8 and 9)

Lesson 6

C & S: CONSEQUENCES AND SEQUEL

C & S = Consequences and Sequel

The invention of the gasoline engine made possible automobiles, airplanes, the oil industry, and a great deal of pollution. If all the consequences could have been foreseen at the time, electric or steam engines might have been used in cars. A new invention, a plan, a rule, or a decision all have consequences that go on for a long time.

An important part of the process of thinking about an action is to focus attention on the future. The consequences should always be considered:

1. Immediate consequences
2. Short-term consequences   (1–5 years)
3. Medium-term consequences   (5–25 years)
4. Long-term consequences   (over 25 years)

The definitions of immediate, short-term, medium-term, and long-term can vary depending on the situation. For example, *immediate* in relation to changing fashions could be this week and *short-term* could be a few months. If the consequences relate to the consideration of a new nuclear power plant, however, *immediate* could be three years and *short-term* could be ten years. Whenever you do a **C & S**, be sure to decide on a definition of the time spans involved.

EXAMPLE: DOING A C & S

A new electronic robot is invented to replace all human labor in factories. The invention is announced.

1. Immediate consequences: Workers worry about their jobs. There might be massive unemployment.
2. Short-term consequences: There might be a shift of work into more service areas. People would be retrained. The method of paying people for their work might change.
3. Medium-term consequences: People might have to take turns at some jobs since there are more people than jobs. There might be two or more people for every job. People might get bored. They might have to take up more hobbies or crafts. People might read more.
4. Long-term consequences: People might work only a few months a year. The whole economy might change.

C & S PRACTICE: SMALL GROUP ACTIVITIES

Use small group procedures to do a **C & S** on each of the following items. For any given item, each group should focus on one type of consequence—immediate, short-term, medium-term, or long-term.

1.   A new law has been suggested to allow schoolchildren to leave school and start earning a living as soon as they want to after the age of twelve. Do a **C & S** on this idea from the point of view of someone who leaves school early, from the point of view of the schools, and from the point of view of society in general.

2.   A new device makes it possible to tell whenever someone is telling a lie. Do a **C & S** on this device.

3.   While an employee is away on vacation, his best friend is promoted to the supervisor's position. His friend has less experience than he does. What do you think will happen when the employee gets back?

4.   Some new medical evidence suggests that people who are slightly overweight are healthier and more productive than people who are underweight. What consequences do you think this evidence will have?

DISCUSS THE C & S PROCESS

1.   Do long-term consequences matter? Why?

2.   If it is not easy to see the consequences, should you bother with them? Why?

3.   When is it most useful to look at consequences?

4.   Whose business is it to look at consequences?

DISCUSS C & S PRINCIPLES

Discuss the items below in class. Which principle do you think is most important? Can you think of any others?

1. Other people may be able to see the consequences of your action more easily than you can yourself. Why?

2. It is important to know whether the consequences are reversible or not. Explain.

3. The immediate consequences and the long-term consequences may be opposite: immediate consequences may be good and long-term consequences bad, or the other way around. Discuss.

4. You should look at consequences not only as they affect you but as they affect other people as well. Why?

5. You should do a full C & S before deciding which changes to consider. Why is this so?

C & S PROJECT 1

Select one of the following items. Write the immediate, short-term, medium-term, and long-term consequences in the space provided.

1. The world runs out of oil and gas. What would happen?

2. All school examinations are abolished. What are the consequences?

Immediate consequences: _____

_____

_____

_____

_____

Short-term consequences: _____

_____

_____

_____

_____

Medium-term consequences: _____

_____

_____

_____

_____

Long-term consequences: _____

_____

_____

_____

_____

C & S PROJECT 2

Select one of the following items. Write the immediate, short-term, medium-term, and long-term consequences in the space provided.

1. What are the consequences of arguing with your teachers?

2. A law is passed banning all imported automobiles. What would happen?

Immediate consequences: _____

_____

_____

_____

Short-term consequences: _____

_____

_____

_____

Medium-term consequences: _____

_____

_____

_____

Long-term consequences: _____

_____

_____

_____

Lesson 7

C & S IN GENERAL BUSINESS

C & S PRACTICE: SMALL GROUP ACTIVITIES

Use small group procedures to do a **C & S** on each of the following items. For any given item, each group should focus on one type of consequence: immediate, short-term, medium-term, or long-term.

1. A short time ago in a quiet residential district, offices started to open. Now there are more and more offices. What will change? Do an immediate and short-term **C & S** on the situation.

2. The price of houses and condominiums rises to the point where young people cannot afford to buy them. What do you think will happen? Do a full **C & S**.

3. Every week, a medium-sized company orders enough computer paper for the next week. Since the company prepares several very large reports and distributes them to everyone in the company, they use a great deal of paper. The purchasing department decides to order a fullyear's supply in order to get a slight discount. What will be the immediate and short-term consequences?

4. A graduate of a food technologies course at a technical college has been offered a sales position for a food ingredient company. The company offers her several options regarding the position. Do a **C & S** on each pair of options.

   a. Salary (the same wages every week) or commission (the only pay is a % of what is sold)
   b. A modest health and life insurance plan paid by the company or a full plan paid one-half by the company and one-half by the employee
   c. A company car or a car allowance for use of the employee's car on the job
   d. A well-defined sales area or freedom to sell anywhere in the country

5. Because of a downturn in the economy, the rural electrical cooperative finds that many people, especially farmers, are falling behind on paying their electric bills. The cooperative proposes to disconnect the electrical service to any user whose payment is seventy-five days or more overdue. Do a full **C & S** on this proposal.

USING C & S IN GENERAL BUSINESS

Use the space provided to record your responses.

1. In business, who should be looking at the consequences of proposed changes?

_____

_____

_____

2. Why is it important to know if the consequences of proposed changes are reversible or not?

_____

_____

_____

_____

3. When is it most important for businesses to consider long-term consequences?

_____

_____

_____

4. How would it be beneficial to review a decision or a course of action to see if the actual result is the same as the consequences that were expected?

_____

_____

_____

_____

C & S PROJECT 1

Select one of the following items. List the consequences that should be considered.

1. A large department store that has been experiencing a lot of shoplifting decides to conduct an all-store inventory. For two days all of the salesclerks spend most of their time counting the items in their departments and then putting the information on an inventory form. Do an immediate and short-term **C & S** on the store's decision.

2. A company that delivers goods is having difficulty getting its customers to pay for the service. The company is running low on cash, but it still must pay its bills and employees. A decision is made that instead of billing customers and waiting for them to pay, the company will have the drivers collect for the service when they pick up the goods. What will be the immediate and short-term consequences of this decision for the company, for the shippers of the goods, and for the receivers of the goods?

Immediate consequences: _____

_____

_____

_____

_____

_____

_____

Short-term consequences: _____

_____

_____

_____

_____

_____

_____

_____

C & S PROJECT 2

Select one of the following items. List the consequences that should be considered.

1. A manufacturer pours its chemical wastes into the river behind the factory. The state has given it notice that it has six months to find a new way to dispose of its wastes. Changing equipment and procedures would be extremely costly, so the company decides to use the six months to find another river location in a different state and move. Meanwhile, they continue to dump their wastes into the river. Do a **C & S** on their decision.

2. A medium-sized grocery store is losing customers. Several very large grocery stores with huge selections and low prices are open twenty-four hours a day. The number of convenience stores is also growing. The owners of the store have decided to focus on service. They plan to mail a list of the items in the store and their prices to every household within three miles. For an extra charge of $2.00 per order, the store will take an order over the telephone and deliver the groceries at a time that is convenient for the customer. Do a **C & S** on the store's decision.

Immediate consequences: _____

_____

_____

_____

Short-term consequences: _____

_____

_____

_____

Medium-term consequences: _____

_____

_____

_____

Long-term consequences: _____

_____

_____

_____

AGO: AIMS, GOALS, OBJECTIVES

AGO = Aims, Goals, Objectives

You can do something out of habit, or because everyone else is doing it, or as a reaction to a situation. These are all "because" reasons. But there are also times when you do something "in order to" achieve some purpose or objective. You can improve your thinking and your decisions if you know exactly what you are trying to achieve. You can also understand other people's thinking better if you see their objectives. In this lesson and the next one you will examine a number of different situations and the goals that affect them. (In certain situations the words *aims* and *goals* are more appropriate than *objectives*, but for our purposes the meaning is the same.)

EXAMPLE: DOING AN AGO

A developer who is building a large new shopping center has the following objectives:

1. To make a profit for his company

2. To make money for himself

3. To build a successful shopping center

4. To build a shopping center that will be approved by the authorities

5. To work so economically and efficiently that he will be asked to develop other shopping centers

Can you think of any others?

AGO PRACTICE: SMALL GROUP ACTIVITIES

Use small group procedures to do an **AGO** on each of the following items.

1. A father is very angry with his daughter, so he doubles her allowance. Why do you think he did this?

2. What would your objectives be if you won $5,000 on a game show?

3. Do an **AGO** for the city police.

4. You are the commander of a spacecraft approaching Earth from another planet. What different objectives might you have?

5. What are your objectives when you turn on the TV?

6. A high school student two years from graduation thinks about the future after high school. Do an **AGO** for the student. How will the goals the student sets affect the student's choice of courses?

DISCUSS THE **AGO** PROCESS

1. Is it always necessary to know your objectives exactly?

2. When is it most useful to know the objectives?

3. What happens if you do not have objectives?

4. How important are other people's objectives?

DISCUSS **AGO** PRINCIPLES

1. If you know exactly what your objectives are, it is easier to achieve them. Why?

2. In the same situation different people may have different objectives. Why? Can you think of an example?

3. On the way to a final objective, there may be a chain of smaller objectives, each one following from the previous one. Why?

4. Objectives should be near enough, real enough, and possible enough for a person to try to reach them. Why?

5. Although there may be many objectives, some are more important than others. Do you agree or disagree? Why?

AGO PROJECT 1

Select one of the following items. Record your responses in the spaces provided.

1. What is the difference between the **AGO** of a politician and the **AGO** of a business executive? List the aims, goals, and objectives; then identify points of difference and points of similarity.

2. Do an **AGO** for a high school principal.

AGO: _____

_____

_____

_____

_____

_____

_____

_____

_____

_____

_____

_____

_____

_____

_____

_____

_____

_____

AGO PROJECT 2

Select one of the following items. Record your responses in the spaces provided.

1. You have just won a lottery and will receive $63,000 per year for twenty years. Do an **AGO** on spending the money.

2. You are setting out to design a completely new type of house. Do an **AGO** for your design.

AGO: _____

_____

_____

_____

_____

_____

_____

_____

_____

_____

_____

_____

_____

_____

_____

_____

AGO IN GENERAL BUSINESS

AGO PRACTICE: SMALL GROUP ACTIVITIES

In small groups, do an **AGO** on each of the following items.

1. Everyone has to eat to live. But people have different objectives with regard to food. Do an **AGO** for the following people: homemaker, cook, store owner, data entry clerk, food manufacturer, farmer.

2. You are a dealer who sells Ford cars. Another Ford dealer in a nearby town lowers her prices so that they are below yours. What are you going to do? What are your objectives?

3. You want to design a new type of car. What are your objectives?

USING **AGO** IN GENERAL BUSINESS

Use the space provided to record your responses.

1. Why is it important for businesses to identify their objectives?

    _____

    _____

    _____

    _____

2. Two companies in the same line of business have different objectives. How can this be? Can you think of any examples?

    _____

    _____

    _____

    _____

3. Why is it important to set smaller objectives that people can reach on their way to reaching a major objective?

    _____

    _____

    _____

    _____

AGO PROJECT 1

Select one of the following items. Use the space provided to write your **AGO.**

1. Janice decides to put in extra time at work, even though her boss told her that she will not get paid for the additional hours. Do an **AGO** on Janice's objectives.

2. Loras is a town in Minnesota. There is only one main street and the population is very small. Nonetheless, there are *two* grocery stores in town, one across the street from the other. The two stores are similar in size and merchandise, but one is owned by Helen and Al whose families have lived in Loras all their lives, while the other is owned by a large corporation that has stores all over the state. What do you think are some of Helen's and Al's objectives? What do you think are some of the objectives of the corporation? Which objectives are the same for the two owners? Which are different?

AGO: _____

_____

_____

_____

_____

_____

_____

_____

_____

_____

_____

_____

_____

_____

AGO PROJECT 2

Select one of the following items. Use the space provided to write your **AGO**.

1. People have different objectives with regard to clothing. Do an **AGO** for the following people: homemaker, student, tailor, dress manufacturer, medical technician, sales representative, plumber, computer programmer, receptionist.

2. Jim just started a training program for insurance sales. He will be paid $125.00 per week while he learns about the insurance business and studies for the tests he must pass to be licensed to sell insurance in his state. After the training, Jim's earnings will be based entirely on how much insurance he sells. Do an **AGO** for Jim while in training and then an **AGO** for his first year selling insurance.

AGO:_____

_____

_____

_____

_____

_____

_____

_____

_____

_____

_____

_____

_____

_____

_____

Lesson 10

PLANNING

Planning is thinking ahead to see how you are going to do something. It may be a matter of getting to some place or of getting something done or it may be a matter of organizing things so that they run smoothly. In a plan, you set up a program of what you are going to do. The more complicated the thing you are going to do, the more necessary it is to have a clear plan.

EXAMPLES

1. A boy plans his vacation.

2. A football coach plans how he is going to win a game.

3. A family plans a picnic.

4. A railway manager plans how to organize the train schedule.

5. A girl plans her career when she leaves school.

PLANNING PRACTICE: SMALL GROUP ACTIVITIES

Use small group procedures for each of the following items.

1. The center of a town has become a slum and the town council wants to do something about it. What are the factors involved and what objectives should the council have? Do a **CAF** and an **AGO** for the town council.

2. In item 1, what plan should the council make? Put the plan into three stages.

3. Do a short-term and a medium-term **C & S** on the plan you made in item 2.

4. Your objective is to make money and you can choose any three of the things listed here: five bicycles, a horse, 2,000 old books, one ton of red paint, a printing machine, and a recipe for sausages. Make a plan showing how you would use your choices.

5. Devise a plan that would make it easier for people to find the jobs they like.

DISCUSS THE PLANNING PROCESS

1. What is difficult about planning?

2.   When are plans necessary?

3. What is the most important thing about planning?

4. What are the disadvantages of having a plan?

DISCUSS PLANNING PRINCIPLES

1. In planning it is important to know exactly what you want to achieve (**AGO**). Why?

2. Always have an alternative plan ready in case something goes wrong with the first plan. Discuss.

3. The value of a plan depends upon its consequences (**C & S**). Explain.

4. Keep the plan as simple and direct as possible. Why?

5. Consider all factors (**CAF**) very carefully and get as much information as possible before making your plan. Why?

PLANNING PROJECT 1

Select one of the following projects. Record your responses in the space provided.

1. You receive permission to turn the school into a no-alcohol nightclub some evenings. Make a plan showing how you would do it; also do a **PMI** on the idea.

2. Large footprints in the snow in the Himalayas are supposed to be due to a mysterious creature called a yeti. Plan an expedition to find out more about the yeti and photograph it if possible.

3. How would you prevent people from hijacking aircraft? Do a **CAF** on hijacking prevention. Can you devise a plan to prevent hijacking?

Plan: _____

_____

_____

_____

_____

_____

_____

_____

_____

_____

_____

_____

_____

_____

_____

PLANNING PROJECT 2

Select one of the following projects. Record your responses in the space provided.

1. You agree to sell candles to raise money for charity and to make some money for yourself. What factors would you have to consider? How would you plan to do this?

2. Your job is to plan the local bus schedule between a busy downtown area and the major suburbs. Do a **CAF** on this project, and then an **AGO**. Can you devise a plan that meets the objectives you identified?

Plan:_____

_____

_____

_____

_____

_____

_____

_____

_____

_____

_____

_____

_____

_____

BREADTH

UNIT 3
FIP: First Important Priorities (Lessons 11 and 12)
APC: Alternatives, Possibilities, Choices (Lessons 13 and 14)

FIP: FIRST IMPORTANT PRIORITIES

FIP = First Important Priorities

Some things are more important than others. Some factors are more important than others. Some objectives are more important than others. Some consequences are more important than others. In thinking about a situation, after you have generated a number of ideas, you have to decide which ones are more important so you can do something about them. After doing a **PMI, CAF, AGO** or **C & S**, you can do a **FIP** to pick out the most important points: the ones you give priority and deal with first.

EXAMPLE: DOING A FIP

Recall that factors identified in the **CAF** example related to buying a car included the following:

1. That the person selling the car actually owns it
2. Price of the car
3. Type of car and the color
4. Engine power and speed of the car
5. Condition of the mechanical parts
6. Size

A race car enthusiast selects engine power and speed as his most important priority. A family with eight children selects size as the most important. A person who wants basic transportation to drive a short distance but has very little money available selects price as most important.

FIP PRACTICE: SMALL GROUP ACTIVITIES

Use small group procedures to do a **FIP** on each of the following items.

1. Do an **AGO** on buying clothes and then do a **FIP** on your objectives.

2. When people vote to elect a politician, what do you think their priorities should be? Do an **AGO** and list four priorities.

3. If you were organizing a party, what would you consider as factors? What would your priorities be?

4. A nineteen-year-old boy wants to spend a year traveling around Africa. He asks his parents for some money. What should their priorities be in deciding whether to help him or not?

5. In deciding whether you like someone or not, which factors do you think are the most important? What are your top three priorities?

DISCUSS THE **FIP** PROCESS

1. Are priorities natural or should you make a special effort to choose them?

2. Are priorities always obvious?

3. When is it most useful to find priorities?

4. How do you choose priorities?

DISCUSS **FIP** PRINCIPLES

1. It is important to get as many ideas as possible first and then to start choosing priorities. Explain.

2. People may have different priorities in the same situation. How can this be done? Can you think of some examples?

3. You should know why you have chosen something as a priority. Why?

4. If it is difficult to choose the most important things, then look at a situation from the other direction: drop the least important and see what is left. How does this help?

5. Ideas not chosen as priorities must also be considered — but after the priorities. Do you agree? Explain.

FIP PROJECT 1

Select one of the following items. Use the space below to record your response.

1. In doing a **CAF** on choosing a career, you may come up with the following factors: the pay, the chances of improvement or promotion, the people you would work with, the work environment, the distance you would have to travel to get to work, the interest or enjoyment of the work. Write an **AGO** for each factor. If you had to pick the three top priorities from these factors, which would you choose? Do a **FIP** on the factors.

2. In running a small business, what are the objectives? What do you think the priorities should be?

FIP: _____

_____

_____

_____

_____

_____

_____

_____

_____

_____

_____

_____

_____

FIP PROJECT 2

Select one of the following items. Use the space below to record your response.

1. The following are types of compensation and benefits a company might provide its employees:

    Salary (the same wage every week)
    Commission (pay based on how much you sell for the company)
    Hourly wages plus overtime pay after forty hours per week
    Flexible work schedule
    Medical insurance
    Dental insurance
    Life insurance
    Disability income insurance (continues to pay you if you can no longer work)
    Profit-sharing (when the company makes a profit, all employees get a share)
    Company savings plan
    Paid vacation
    Paid holidays
    Company uniforms or clothing allowance

Do the following **FIP**: Assign each item a number from 1 to 13, 1 being most important and 13 the least, according to how important the items are to you in your consideration of a job.

2. If you were in charge of distributing money for medical research, how would you choose to divide the money? What factors would you consider? What would your priorities be?

FIP: _____

_____

_____

_____

_____

_____

_____

_____

_____

_____

Lesson 12

FIP IN GENERAL BUSINESS

FIP PRACTICE: SMALL GROUP ACTIVITIES

In small groups, do a **FIP** on each of the following items.

1. Do an **AGO** on the goals of a tape and video store; then do a **FIP** on the store's objectives. Do the same for an employee of the store. In what ways are the **FIP**s of the store and the employees similar? How are they different?

2. Your company likes to develop its employees and promote them within the company. For instance, a purchasing secretary could be promoted to purchasing clerk, then purchasing agent. When hiring a new secretary, some factors to be considered are related to immediate job performance. Others are related to promotability. Do a **CAF** that identifies factors for *both* of these areas. Then do a **FIP** for each group of factors.

3. Do a **CAF** on the factors regarding selecting a location for your new candy store. Do a **FIP** on these factors.

USING **FIP** IN GENERAL BUSINESS

Use the space provided to record your responses.

1. Why does a business need to identify its priorities?

_____

_____

_____

_____

2. How does a business determine its most important priorities? How is the procedure different from an individual deciding on priorities?

_____

_____

_____

_____

_____

_____

3. Many businesses write a formal business plan and update it every year. Part of the plan is a clear statement of which objectives are most important to the business (the company's **FIP**). How is this important on a day-to-day basis to people working for the company? How does it help to know the company's objectives and **FIPs**?

_____

_____

_____

_____

_____

_____

4. How can a company be certain that employees know its priorities? How can employees tell management about factors that may be important enough to change company priorities?

_____

_____

_____

_____

_____

_____

5. Are there different priorities for different departments in the same company? Why?

_____

_____

_____

_____

_____

_____

6. What factors can lead a company to change its priorities?

_____

_____

_____

_____

_____

_____

_____

FIP PROJECT 1

Select one of the following items. Use the space provided to record your **AGO** and **FIP**.

1. A bicycle company is not meeting its goal of selling fifteen percent more bicycles than last year. This goal was the number-one priority for the sales department. Do a **CAF** on what may be contributing to the problem. Do an **AGO** to determine the objectives for sales representatives in their individual efforts. Then do a **FIP** on the objectives you identify.

2. Your company is considering buying an automatic widget maker that can make widgets much faster with fewer people. Do an **AGO** on purchasing the new machine. Do a **FIP** for the objectives you identify.

AGO:_____

_____

_____

_____

_____

_____

_____

FIP:_____

_____

_____

_____

_____

_____

_____

_____

FIP PROJECT 2

Select one of the following items. Use the space provided to record your response.

1. Your company bottles soft drinks. You are considering a change from glass bottles to plastic bottles. Do a **CAF** on the change. Do a **FIP** to determine the most important factors. If the government enacts a tough recycling law that bans disposable containers, how will this affect your priorities? When a government regulation is one of the factors in your **CAF**, where does it fit in your **FIP**?

2. Your company's **FIP** lists four priorities:

    a. Make the highest quality product possible in its price range
    b. Make a profit from the sale of the product; that is, sell the product for more than it costs to make it
    c. Share the profits with the employees through a profit-sharing program
    d. Share the profits with the community through charitable giving

If the company has a year with little or no profit, does that change the company's **FIP**? Explain.

_____

_____

_____

_____

_____

_____

_____

_____

_____

_____

_____

APC: ALTERNATIVES, POSSIBILITIES, CHOICES

APC = Alternatives, Possibilities, Choices

When you have to make a decision or take action, you may at first think that you do not have any choices. But if you look for them, you may find that there are more alternatives than you thought. Similarly, in looking at a situation there are always obvious explanations. But if you look more closely, you may find that there are other possible explanations that you had not thought of.

EXAMPLE: DOING AN APC

A car is found in a ditch and the driver is dead. What could have happened?

1. The driver had a heart attack or fainted.

2. The car had a puncture, blowout, or mechanical failure.

3. The driver was drunk.

4. The driver misjudged the curve of the road.

5. The driver was attacked by a wasp and lost concentration.

6. The driver fell asleep.

7. The driver was murdered and then placed in the crashed car.

APC PRACTICE: SMALL GROUP ACTIVITIES

Use small group procedures to do an **APC** on each of the following items.

1. You discover that your coworker is a thief. What alternatives do you have?

2. The Post Office is losing a lot of money. If you were running it, what alternatives would you have?

3. The best data entry clerk in the information department starts making mistakes intentionally. What possible explanations are there?

4. Fewer people want to be truck drivers. What are the possible explanations for this and what possible actions could be taken to avoid a shortage of drivers?

5. You want to get to sleep but a neighbor is playing loud music. Do an **APC** on your alternatives. 1) What can you do at the time? 2) What can you do to prevent the situation from happening again?

DISCUSS THE **APC** PROCESS

1. What is the point of looking for more alternatives?

2. How do you tell which is the most likely or best alternative?

3. When do you stop looking for other possibilities?

4. When is it most useful to find new choices?

DISCUSS **APC** PRINCIPLES

1. If you cannot think of any alternatives yourself, you should ask someone else. Why?

2. Continue to look for alternatives until you find one that you really like. Why?

3.   There is almost always an alternative, even if there does not appear to be one at first. How do you find it?

4. You cannot know that the obvious explanation is best until you have looked at other possible explanations. Why is this so?

5. To look for alternatives when you are not satisfied is easy, but to look for them when you are satisfied requires deliberate effort. Do you agree? Explain.

APC PROJECT 1

Select one of the following items. Use the space provided to record your **APC**.

1. A factory owner knows that if she pays the wages her workers demand and probably deserve, she will lose money and will have to close the factory. Unemployment would occur in the area. What choices does she have?

2. A young man wants to take a job in a nearby town, but he has to stay at home to look after his aging father. What alternatives does he have?

APC: _____

_____

_____

_____

_____

_____

_____

_____

_____

_____

_____

_____

_____

_____

_____

_____

APC PROJECT 2

Select one of the following items. Use the space provided to record your **APC**.

1. In dealing with pollution from a factory, what alternative courses of action are there?

2. A manufacturer of personal computers is steadily losing sales to foreign imports. What explanations and choices are there?

APC: _____

_____

_____

_____

_____

_____

_____

_____

_____

_____

_____

_____

_____

_____

_____

Lesson 14

<u>APC</u> IN GENERAL BUSINESS

APC PRACTICE: SMALL GROUP ACTIVITIES

In small groups, do an **APC** on each of the following items.

1. Your company makes toys, most of which are sold for Christmas gifts. One of your toys seems to be the hit of the year, but you do not have enough for all the stores that want it. What are your alternatives?

2. Your boss repeatedly asks you to perform personal errands that are not related to your job. You do not feel that you should have to run the errands but worry that you will lose your job if you refuse. Do an **APC** to identify your alternatives.

3. Your business has doubled in the past three years. You have many new employees and seem to have lost the family feeling the company once had. Rumors say that the new employees are considering forming a union to demand higher wages and benefits. Do an **APC** for this situation.

USING APC IN GENERAL BUSINESS

Use the space provided to record your responses.

1. In a business, responsibilities are divided among departments and people. Each person knows about his or her area of responsibility and makes daily decisions based on this knowledge. How can a company best do an **APC** on a major decision affecting the entire company?

    _____

    _____

    _____

    _____

    _____

    _____

2. In a business, is it important for a supervisor to involve the people in his or her department in the **APC** process? Why? How can this be done? What is a good way for an employee to tell a supervisor about a new alternative for the way the department does its work? Think of ways to present an alternative to which the supervisor probably will *not* be receptive.

    _____

    _____

    _____

    _____

    _____

    _____

    _____

    _____

APC PROJECT 1

Select one of the following items. Use the space provided to write your **APC**.

1. Your company has pipe in stock that it cannot sell. The pipe is in good condition, but no customers have ordered this size for four years. Do an **APC** on what to do with the pipe.

2. You work for an airline. You're at the gate where passengers board the plane, and it is apparent that the airline has sold more tickets than there are seats available and some people will not get on the flight. Some passengers are becoming very upset. Do an **APC** for dealing with this situation.

APC: _____

_____

_____

_____

_____

_____

_____

_____

_____

_____

_____

_____

_____

_____

_____

APC PROJECT 2

Select one of the following items. Use the space provided to write your **APC**.

1. You work in a word processing pool at a large company. The sales department has many long documents that must be prepared in order to get orders for the coming year. Several employees are on vacation and not all the documents can be typed on time. Do an **APC** on the situation.

2. A taxicab company decides to enforce a dress and appearance code that requires drivers to be neatly dressed and groomed. The drivers object to this code. Do an **APC** to identify alternatives that the drivers have and those of the taxicab company.

APC: _____

_____

_____

_____

_____

_____

_____

_____

_____

_____

_____

_____

_____

_____

Lesson 15

DECISIONS

Some decisions are easy and some are difficult. There are decisions to be made all the time: which clothes to wear, which tapes to buy, whether to go out or not, how to amuse yourself, which career to choose, whether to stay in a job or not, whether to travel, whether to spend money on something or save it. Sometimes the decision is a choice between alternatives. Sometimes the decision is forced on you; for example, you come to a fork in the road and have to decide which road to take. In making decisions it is useful to be clear about the factors involved (**CAF**), the objectives (**AGO**), the priorities (**FIP**), the consequences (**C & S**), and the alternatives (**APC**).

DECISION PRACTICE: SMALL GROUP ACTIVITIES

Use small group procedures for each of the following items.

1. You are offered $100 now or $200 in a year's time. How would you decide between the two? Explain the reasons behind your decisions. Do a **C & S** on both choices.

2. A restaurant owner has two candidates for a job serving customers: one candidate is quiet and rather homely, but hardworking; the other is better looking and more fun but rather unreliable. Both want the job. The owner has to decide. Do a **C & S** on both choices. Now do an **APC** for the owner.

3. Parents with a deaf child have to decide whether to send her to a special school or to an ordinary school. Do an **AGO** for the parents; do an **FIP** on the objectives. Are there other alternatives?

4. An employee in a meat packing company has to decide on whether to let his co-workers know he dances in a ballet group. Do an **AGO** for the employee. Do a **C & S** on telling his coworkers.

5. A new graduate from a technical college has a choice of two jobs. How can the graduate decide which to take? Do a **CAF** for the graduate. Do a **FIP** on the factors.

6. A local printing company will not employ spouses. Two employees have become attracted to one another, dated, and now wish to marry. They are afraid one of them will lose his or her job. How do they decide what to do? What thinking tools could they apply? Select the appropriate tools and use their procedures.

70

DISCUSS THE DECISION PROCESS

1. Why are some decisions easier to make than others?

2. What are the most important things to think about in making a decision?

3. How can you tell that the decision you have made is the right one?

4. Is it better to think about decisions or just to make them and see what happens?

DISCUSS DECISION PRINCIPLES

1. You should always be able to tell yourself the real reason behind any decision you make. Explain.

2. It is important to know whether a decision can be reversed after it has been made. Why is this important?

3. Not making a decision is really a decision to do nothing. Why?

4. Decisions are difficult to make if you are not prepared to give up something in order to gain something. How is this so?

5. In making a decision, consider all the factors (**CAF**), look at the consequences (**C & S**), be clear about objectives (**AGO**), assess the priorities (**FIP**), and find all the possible alternatives (**APC**). When you have done this, a decision may be much easier. Why?

DECISION PROJECT 1

Select one of the following projects. Use the space provided to record your response.

1. The kidnappers of a banker demand a large amount of money for her release. The police know that if the money is paid, then other people will be kidnapped for money. If the money is not paid, the banker will not be released. How should the police make a decision?

2. A city housing officer thinks that if he finds homes for the homeless in his town, then homeless people in other areas will hear of this and move into the town, and the problem will never be solved. What can he decide?

3. How does a company decide to spend its money?

Decision process_____

_____

_____

_____

_____

_____

_____

_____

_____

_____

_____

_____

_____

_____

DECISION PROJECT 2

Select one of the following projects. Use the space provided to record your response.

1. An employee in your company has a drug-dependency problem. How can the company decide about how to respond to the problem?

2. In any purchasing department, there are always decisions to be made on supplies or materials to be purchased. Higher quality costs more. Lower costs may mean lower quality. How can decisions be made?

3. Advances in technology require changes for some employees. Many employees will be retrained, but some jobs may be eliminated. How should a company make decisions about adding higher technology and retraining or eliminating employees?

Decision process:_____

_____

_____

_____

_____

_____

_____

_____

_____

_____

_____

_____

_____

_____

Part Two

INTERACTION

Skills that improve your thinking in situations involving other people, such as arguments, debates, and negotiations.

OPV: Other People's Views (Lessons 16 and 17)
EBS: Examine Both Sides (Lesson 18)
ADI: Agreement, Disagreement, Irrelevance (Lesson 19)

OPV: OTHER PEOPLE'S VIEWS

OPV = Other People's Views

Many thinking situations involve other people. What other people think is just as much part of a situation as the factors, consequences, or objectives. Other people may have very different viewpoints. Although they are in the same situation, they may look at things differently. An important part of thinking is understanding how other people are thinking. Doing an **OPV** is about seeing things from another person's viewpoint. Another person may consider different factors (**CAF**), see different consequences (**C & S**), and have different objectives (**AGO**) or priorities (**FIP**).

EXAMPLE: DOING AN OPV

A salesperson is trying to sell you a used sports car. The salesperson's point of view is that the engine is powerful, the tires are new, the car suits you, and it is a good buy. Your point of view is that you must determine whether it has been in a crash, how much spare tires cost, how worn the parts are, how much gas it uses, and how it compares to other cars you have seen.

OPV PRACTICE: SMALL GROUP ACTIVITIES

Use small group procedures to do an **OPV** on each of the following items.

1. A company president gives notice that, starting in sixty days, smoking will no longer be allowed on the premises. Do an **OPV** for smokers, nonsmokers, the personnel manager, and the company president.

2. An inventor discovers a new way of making cloth. This invention means that only one person of every twenty would still be employed in making cloth. Do an **OPV** for the inventor, factory owners, the workers, and the general public.

3. During a train and bus strike people find it difficult to get to work. What are the different points of view involved in this situation?

4. A worker refuses to obey his foreman. The foreman reports the employee to the plant supervisor, who suspends him. The worker's union objects and files a complaint against the foreman. What are the viewpoints of the worker, the foreman, the plant supervisor, the union representative, and the coworkers?

DISCUSS THE OPV PROCESS

1. Is it easy to see other viewpoints?

2. Whose point of view is right if points of view differ?

3. If other people cannot see your point of view, should you bother about theirs?

4. Why is it necessary to see someone else's viewpoint?

5. Should your actions be based on your own viewpoint or someone else's as well?

DISCUSS OPV PRINCIPLES

1. You ought to be able to see other points of view whether you agree with them or not. How is this helpful?

2. Every point of view may be right for the person holding it, but not right enough to be imposed on others. Discuss.

3. Different people have different positions, backgrounds, knowledge, interests, values, wants, and so on; it is not surprising, therefore, that in the same situation viewpoints may differ greatly. Can you think of some examples?

4. It is important to determine whether the other person can see your viewpoint. Why?

5. How is being able to articulate the differences and similarities among viewpoints helpful?

OPV PROJECT 1

Select one of the following items. Use the space provided to record your **OPV**.

1. A lawyer is defending in court a company that she believes to be guilty of supplying faulty automotive brake components. What are the viewpoints of the lawyer, the judge, the accused company, owners of automobiles with the brake parts, and the jury?

2. A plan is under way to pull down some old houses and build modern factories with wider roads between them. What are the viewpoints of the city planners, the architects, the adults and children who live in the houses, and the companies that want the new factories? Do a **C & S** from the viewpoint of the residents and one from the viewpoint of the companies that want the new factories.

OPV: _____

_____

_____

_____

_____

_____

_____

_____

_____

_____

_____

_____

_____

_____

_____

_____

OPV PROJECT 2

Select one of the following items. Use the space provided to write your **OPV**.

1. Many people talk about pollution, but cleaning up the environment costs money. What are the viewpoints of an ordinary citizen, an environmental group, industrialists, and the government?

2. Due to a shortage of a new, popular sports car, automobile dealerships are adding as much as $2,000 to the price of the car. What are the viewpoints of the owner of the dealership, the sales representatives at the dealership, buyers of the cars, and the manufacturer of the cars?

OPV:_____

_____

_____

_____

_____

_____

_____

_____

_____

_____

_____

_____

_____

_____

_____

OPV IN GENERAL BUSINESS

OPV PRACTICE: SMALL GROUP ACTIVITIES

In small groups, do an OPV on each of the following items.

1. Reconstruction of an aging freeway through the center of a large city will disrupt traffic for months. A plan is being considered that would give the contractor bonuses for finishing early and penalties for finishing late. What are the viewpoints of the contractor, motorists who use the freeway, taxpayers whose money is used for payment, and lawmakers who need to approve the plan?

2. A strike turned violent. Local law enforcement agencies could not prevent damage to the company's factory. The governor has called out the National Guard to prevent further incidents. What are the viewpoints of the factory owners, striking workers, a non-union supervisor in the factory, a local police officer, a member of the National Guard, and the spouse of a striker?

3. A toy manufacturer cannot keep up with orders for its newest toy. Overtime work has been scheduled for the Friday, Saturday, and Sunday after Thanksgiving to try to get more toys made in time for Christmas. What are the viewpoints of the factory workers, the plant manager, the sales manager, the stores that sell toys, consumers who buy toys, children who receive toys?

USING **OPV** IN GENERAL BUSINESS

Use the space provided to record your responses.

1. Each department within a company may represent a different viewpoint. How do people in one
    department learn the views of people in other departments? Is it important that departments
    know each other's viewpoint? Why? Who in the company must resolve differences in
    viewpoints among departments?

    _____

    _____

    _____

    _____

    _____

2. Is it important that a supervisor know her employees' viewpoints? When? Why? How can
    differences in viewpoints among employees in a department affect that department's work?
    Must people's viewpoints be the same for them to be able to work well together?

    _____

    _____

    _____

    _____

3. Why is it important for a sales department to know the point of view of the manufacturing
    department? Why? Why should the manufacturing department know the point of view of the
    sales department?

    _____

    _____

    _____

    _____

    _____

OPV PROJECT 1

Select one of the following items. Use the space provided to record your **OPV**.

1. A foreman reports to the safety supervisor: one of his workers has informed him that a coworker is using marijuana on the job. Do an **OPV** for the worker supposedly using marijuana, the worker who reported the drug use to the foreman, the foreman, and the safety supervisor. Do an **AGO** from the point of view of the worker who reported the drug use and from the point of view of the user.

2. A female computer operator thinks her male supervisor is making unwanted and unwelcome sexual comments to her. The supervisor will not stop and the personnel manager refuses to get involved, so she calls the State Attorney General's office and files a complaint. Do an **OPV** for the computer operator, the personnel manager, the attorney who handles sexual harassment complaints for the state, and the president of the company involved.

OPV: _____

_____

_____

_____

_____

_____

_____

_____

_____

_____

_____

_____

_____

OPV PROJECT 2

Select one of the following items. Use the space provided to record your **OPV**.

1. Several women working in an electronics assembly area have complained to their supervisor about a coworker, also a woman. They state that her personal hygiene and body odor are so bad they do not want to work near her. Do an **OPV** for the dirty worker, the coworkers who complained, the coworkers who did not complain, and the supervisor.

2. One rider in a company-sponsored commuter van is not ready to leave on time at least three of five days each week. The reason is that the rider, a single parent, is getting grade school children ready for school each morning. Do an **OPV** for the van driver, the coriders, the late rider, the riders' supervisors, the manager of the company van pool, and the children.

OPV:_____

_____

_____

_____

_____

_____

_____

_____

_____

_____

_____

_____

_____

_____

Lesson *18*

EBS: EXAMINE BOTH SIDES

EBS = **E**xamine **B**oth **S**ides

In doing an **OPV**, we learned to explore other persons' sides, or viewpoints, of an issue or problem. In an argument, disagreement, quarrel, dispute, or debate there are usually two sides. Each side believes that it is right and that the other side is wrong.

Here are three examples: (1) Once upon a time there were people who argued that the earth was flat and others who argued that it was round. (2) At one time some people argued that the earth was the center of the universe and others argued that the sun was the center. (3) Sometimes the workers in a business want more money and management argues that wages cannot be increased further.

In such arguments each side is usually so busy saying what it thinks and why it is right that it never really listens to the arguments of the other side.

In an **EBS** each side examines the other side's arguments so well that one side could present the arguments of the other side if asked to do so.

EXAMPLE: DOING AN EBS

Should the minimum age at which a student can quit school be raised by one year?

Side A: Yes. More education is needed for jobs.
It may be necessary to change jobs later on.
More education makes people happier.
It would help unemployment.

Side B: No. Many students are already too bored at school.
Students could be earning money instead of sitting in class.
School education is not helpful for all jobs.
It is better to learn a job directly by starting sooner.
More schools and teachers would be needed.

Side A should be able to give the exact arguments of Side B if asked to do an **EBS**. Similarly, Side B should be able to give the exact arguments of Side A if asked to do an **EBS**.

EBS PRACTICE: SMALL GROUP ACTIVITIES

The class or group should be divided into two teams. One side must think of all the arguments for Side A; the other side must think of all the arguments for Side B. After you have thought of all the arguments for your side, switch sides and think of the arguments for the other side. Select one of the items below for this activity. If there is time, do both of them.

1. There is evidence that cigarette smoking is dangerous to health and can cause lung cancer, chronic bronchitis, and heart disease. Should smoking be banned by law or should people just be warned about the dangers and allowed to smoke if they want to? Only some people will get the diseases, and the tax from tobacco helps pay for government services. But three times more people die of lung cancer each year than are killed on the roads.

   Side A: Arguments for the complete banning by law of cigarette smoking to show why the present system is not good enough

   Side B: Arguments against the complete banning by law and arguments to show why the present system is better

2. Is it better to live in the country or in a town?

   Side A: Arguments in favor of country living and against city living

   Side B: Arguments in favor of city living and against country living

DISCUSS THE EBS PROCESS

1. Why is it necessary to fully understand both sides of an argument, debate, or negotiation?

2. Is it natural or easy to fully examine two sides?

3. Are most people eager to prove their point? Explain.

DISCUSS EBS PRINCIPLES

1. How is being able to understand and present another side's arguments (to "switch sides") helpful?

2. It is important to determine whether persons on another side of an argument can argue your side. Why?

EBS PROJECT 1

Select one of the following items. Use the space provided to record your response.

1. Some people argue that local industries should be protected from foreign competition. For example, the government might limit the number of foreign cars that can be imported or the quantity of foreign shoes. Others argue that there must be free trade in order to benefit consumers, and if a business cannot compete it should close down.

    Side A: Arguments for protection of local industries

    Side B: Arguments for free trade and no limits on foreign imports

2. In some countries TV broadcasting is limited to a fixed number of hours every day. It is said that people then spend more time reading, talking, and doing their hobbies. In other countries there is almost continuous TV broadcasting.

    Side A: Arguments for limiting the number of hours of TV broadcasting

    Side B: Arguments against restricting TV broadcasting by law and arguments for letting people watch as much TV as they wish

Side A: _____

_____

_____

_____

_____

_____

Side B:_____

_____

_____

_____

_____

_____

EBS PROJECT 2

Select one of the following items. Use the space provided to record your response.

1. In your company the data entry clerks are, as a group, fast and accurate. There has never been
    a problem with the quality or efficiency of their work, although they tend to be talkative and
    casual. The supervisor has just told the clerks that they can no longer have food or beverages
    at their work stations.

    Side A: Arguments for eliminating food and beverages at work stations

    Side B: Arguments for continuing to allow employees to have food and beverages at
              work stations

2. The office workers at Acme Maufacturing have asked the personnel manager to allow them to
    work flexible hours. By this, they mean that they could work any hours or schedule they want
    as long as they work a total of forty hours per week. Although the idea has worked for some
    companies, the personnel manager says that it is not acceptable for Acme Manufacturing.

    Side A: Arguments for flexible hours

    Side B: Arguments for continuing regular, uniform, eight-hour work days.

Side A: _____

_____

_____

_____

_____

_____

Side B: _____

_____

_____

_____

_____

Lesson 19

ADI: AGREEMENT, DISAGREEMENT, IRRELEVANCE

A = **Agreement**   Points on which the two sides agree
D = **Disagreement** Points on which the two sides disagree
I = **Irrelevance**   Points that are irrelevant and do not matter

In an argument the two sides don't disagree about everything. Usually they disagree on some points and agree on others. There may also be points that are so irrelevant that agreement or disagreement does not matter. A deliberate effort should be made to determine the points of agreement, disagreement, and irrelevance by doing an **ADI.**

To do an **ADI**, list the points under **A**, then the points under **D**, and finally the points under **I**.

EXAMPLE: DOING AN ADI

Should there be special company uniforms or should each person wear what he or she likes?

A: Both sides agree that company uniforms

> are more easily recognizable.
> are an added expense for the company.
> remove the bother of wondering what to wear.
> remove the differences in clothing due to income or choice.

D: Side A maintains that ordinary clothing is more comfortable but Side B disagrees.

Side B says that uniforms lead to a greater pride in the company but Side A disagrees.

Side B claims that uniforms are much tidier and safer, but Side A says that this is not always so.

Side A says that worker comfort is more important than the company image, but Side B disagrees and says that the company image is in the worker's own interest.

I: Both Side A and Side B think that the color of the uniform is irrelevant.

Neither Side A nor Side B feels it is relevant to require different color uniforms for different jobs.

89

ADI PRACTICE: SMALL GROUP ACTIVITIES

Use small group procedures for each of the following items.

1. A common argument exists about the effect of TV violence (guns, fights, bombs, and so on) on young people.

    Side A: Claims that so much TV violence must influence young people and make them more violent themselves

    Side B: Disagrees and says that TV only entertains and does not make people do what they would not have done anyway

    The following points arise during the argument. Decide which might be the points of agreement (**A**), the points of disagreement (**D**), and irrelevant points (**I**).

    a. Most people spend four to five hours watching TV each day.
    b. Most programs on TV are realistic and easily imitated.
    c. Violence has always been around in stories, games, books, and so on; its presence on TV is nothing new.
    d. TV has a stronger effect than any other medium.
    e. There is no need for TV to show so much violence.
    f. Violence should only be shown when children are in bed.
    g. Because of TV, people take violence for granted and become casual about it.
    h. People do not regard TV as the real world but as a fairy tale, and you do not imitate fairy tales.
    i. The real world is full of violence, so depicting it on TV helps prepare young people for the real world.

2. Someone has suggested that assembly workers who are faster at getting their work done should work fewer hours per week. Do an **ADI** on the two sides of the argument.

    Side A: Arguments in favor of shorter hours for assembly workers who are faster at getting their jobs done

    Side B: Arguments against shorter hours and in favor of everyone working the same number of hours

DISCUSS THE ADI PROCESS AND PRINCIPLES

1. When is it important to deliberately determine points of agreement, disagreement, and irrelevance by doing an **ADI**?

2. How does doing an **ADI** facilitate compromise?

3. How does identifying irrelevant points help clarify an argument?

ADI PROJECT 1

Select one of the following items. Use the space provided to record an **EBS** for each side of the argument. Then write your **ADI** for the two sides of the argument.

1. Some people have suggested that the government should ensure that everyone gets adequate health care. Companies and individuals would no longer pay directly for health insurance but they would be taxed to pay for medical care for anyone who needs it.

   Side A: Arguments that the proposed change is the only fair way to provide adequate medical care for everyone

   Side B: Arguments that the current system of private insurance with some medical assistance for those who really need it is the best way to meet people's needs

2. It is sometimes claimed that a person who is very hungry and has no money has a right to steal food, for instance from a supermarket.

   Side A: Arguments that stealing is always wrong and a person has no right to steal

   Side B: Arguments that the right to survive is stronger than the right to property

Side A: _____

_____

_____

Side B: _____

_____

_____

A:_____

_____

D:_____

_____

I:_____

_____

ADI PROJECT 2

Think about an issue, situation, or problem related to your job or school about which there is disagreement. Write a clear statement of the problem or issue, then write an **EBS** for each side of the argument. Next write your **ADI** for the two sides of the argument.

Issue:_____

_____

_____

Side A:_____

_____

_____

_____

Side B:_____

_____

_____

_____

A:_____

_____

_____

D:_____

_____

_____

I:_____

_____

_____

INTERACTION REVIEW

The main purpose of this lesson is to practice **OPV**, **EBS**, and **ADI**. **OPV** is a deliberate effort to discover how the viewpoints of people in the same situation may be entirely different. **EBS** is the examination of opposing viewpoints—going beyond the general point of view to more fully explore two sides of a question or issue. **ADI** is used to determine the points of agreement, disagreement, and irrelevance between the two sides of an issue.

EXAMPLE

An automobile manufacturer that has been working on a new sports car finds that there are still some mechanical problems with the test cars. The company must decide whether to produce the car now or delay it.

When we do an **OPV**, we find the following viewpoints:

1. The designer's viewpoint: They have designed a good car and the problems can be worked out in time for production.

2. The safety engineer's viewpoint: If mechanical problems affect safe operation, the car must not be produced.

3. The sales manager's viewpoint: We need this new car in the fall lineup to draw customers into the showroom.

4. The production manager's viewpoint: Making a new car that still has problems will cause even more problems on the production line.

5. The warranty manager's viewpoint: Mechanical breakdowns will lead to expensive warranty repairs.

6. The production worker's viewpoint: We need job security and making a new car will help that.

A strong disagreement about making the new model develops between the sales manager and the manufacturing manager. The sales manager argues yes; the manufacturing manager no. An **EBS** on these positions reveals points on each side.

The sales manager argues yes:

1. Car magazines have featured the car and people want to buy it.

2. Our dealerships want the new model to draw people to the showroom.

3. The company needs the money from selling the new model.

4. Employees can work overtime to get the new car into production.

5. It would be unwise to introduce a car with mechanical defects, but the designers say they can correct the problems. They have done so in the past and we should trust their ability now.

6. If we get the car out this year, we will be a year ahead of a similar model from our competition.

The production manager argues no:

1. The car has mechanical problems and isn't ready for production, and we don't think it can be ready soon.

2. If the problems are not all corrected, warranty repair costs will be high.

3. Changes in design after production starts are expensive and time-consuming.

4. Even if the problems are corrected, there will be little time to set up the production line, and quality might suffer.

5. If production is delayed a year, the new painting area will be completed and the car will have a better finish.

6. It is more important to have the car produced correctly than to have it done quickly.

Doing an **ADI** on those arguments, we find points of agreement, disagreement, and irrelevance.

Agreement:

1. Any mechanical problems must be fixed before production begins.

2. It would be wrong to knowingly sell a new model with mechanical problems.

3. It is financially beneficial to the company to start selling a new model as soon as possible.

Disagreement:

1. Whether the mechanical problems with the car can be corrected in time

2. Whether getting the car out at the start of the new car year is urgent

3. How quickly the production line can be prepared to make the new model

Irrelevance:

1. The updating of production facilities

INTERACTION PROJECT 1

A retail store chain needs to build a bigger warehouse. The warehouse is used to receive large quantities of merchandise from the companies that manufacture the items. The warehouse sends the merchandise to individual stores as needed. The current warehouse and the main office are in a large city, at separate sites. A neighboring state is offering incentives to build the new warehouse in a rural area of that state. A decision must be made to relocate in the same large city or to go to the rural area in the neighboring state.

1. Do an **OPV** on the following: a warehouse worker, the personnel manager, the financial manager, the warehouse manager, the transportation manager (responsible for shipping merchandise in and out of the warehouse), the properties manager (responsible for construction of the new warehouse).

_____

_____

_____

_____

_____

_____

_____

_____

_____

_____

_____

_____

_____

_____

_____

2. The warehouse manager and the transportation manager disagree. The warehouse manager argues for the rural location, the transportation manager for the city. Do an **EBS** on their positions.

_____

_____

_____

_____

_____

_____

_____

3. Examine the points of the two sides of the argument and do an **ADI** on the points.

_____

_____

_____

_____

_____

_____

_____

_____

_____

_____

_____

INTERACTION PROJECT 2

A furniture manufacturing company is evaluating whether or not all employees, regardless of gender, should be allowed up to three months' leave of absence when the employee or the employee's spouse has a child. The employee would receive pay for the first month away from the job.

1. Do an **OPV** for the following: a young employee considering starting a family, an older employee who will have no more children, the personnel manager, the financial manager, the production manager.

_____

_____

_____

_____

_____

_____

_____

_____

_____

2. The personnel manager disagrees with the production manager. The personnel manager argues for the leave, the production manager against it. Do an **EBS** on their arguments.

_____

_____

_____

_____

_____

_____

_____

3. Do an **ADI** on the arguments to examine the conflict.

_____

_____

_____

_____

_____

_____

_____

_____

_____

_____

_____

Part Three

INFORMATION

Skills concerned with eliciting information and assessing it.

UNIT 1
Information (Lessons 21 and 22)
Questions (Lessons 23 and 24)

Lesson **21**

INFORMATION

FI & FO: INFORMATION-IN AND INFORMATION-OUT

FI = Information-**in**
FO = Information-**out**

What we know about something is called information. Sometimes we obtain the information for ourselves and sometimes it is given to us. The information we get or are given tells us things we want to know, but it may also leave out some things we would like to know.

Information-**in** (**FI**)

Information-**in** is the information that is included; the information that has been put in; the information that has been given; what we know.

Information-**out** (**FO**)

Information-**out** is the information that has been left out; the information that is missing; the information that we would like to know.
     Doing an **FI & FO** means looking to see exactly what information has been put in and what has been left out.

EXAMPLE: DOING AN FI & FO

I shall catch the 9 a.m. flight to Chicago on Monday. Please meet me at the airport.

Information-in (FI): The information that is actually given includes

1. The person will be traveling to Chicago on Monday.
2. The person will be outside of Chicago for at least some time on Monday.
3. There is a flight that the person can take to Chicago (the person can get to an airport).
4. There is a 9 a.m. flight.
5. The person expects the flight to be operating.
6. The person has decided to travel by plane.

Information-out (FO): The information that has been left out includes

1. Who the person is
2. The date of the Monday
3. Where the person will be traveling from
4. The airline that will be used
5. The actual time of arrival
6. To whom the message is addressed
7. At which of the Chicago airports the person will arrive

FI & FO PRACTICE: SMALL GROUP ACTIVITIES

Use small group procedures to do an **FI & FO** on each of the following items.

1. A driver is trying to find a town called Hartford. He does not know the way and when he gets to a Y junction he finds that the sign indicating the road to Hartford is lying beside the road. Do an **FI & FO** to determine if there is anything the driver can do.

2. In a travel agent's advertisement you read the following: "An exclusive holiday in the Bahamas. Hotel near the sea. Sail and water-ski. Two weeks including travel." What information has been left out? What else would you like to know?

3. You see an advertisement for a job. "Wanted: men or women to train as assistant store managers. Age: 16-40. Three weeks' vacation a year. Free lunches and free uniform. Competitive rates of pay with bonus." Do an **FI & FO**.

DISCUSS THE **FI & FO** PROCESS

1. Is it always necessary to have 100 percent of the information about something?

2. When is it most useful to do an **FI & FO**?

3. What happens if you accept the information you have and do not determine what information has been left out?

DISCUSS **FI & FO** PRINCIPLES

1. When you carefully examine the information-in (**FI**) you can sometimes reduce the information-out (**FO**). Why?

2. If you know what your objective or your task is, it is easier to do an **FO**. Why? Can you think of examples?

3. Sometimes you have more information in than you need for a specific purpose. Do you agree? Why?

4. Doing an **FO** is more difficult than doing an **FI**. Is this always true?

FI & FO PROJECT 1

Use the space provided below to do an **FI & FO** on one of the following items.

1. You want to set up a children's playground in town. What information should you collect? What information is likely to be left out?

2. Based on the information that you now have, what careers are open to you when you leave school?

FI: _____

_____

_____

_____

_____

_____

_____

FO: _____

_____

_____

_____

_____

_____

_____

_____

FI & FO PROJECT 2

Select one of the following items. Use the space provided to record your **FI & FO**.

1. Your company makes several types of boxes. It sells the boxes in all major cities of the country. The company's computer prints a report every six months that shows how many boxes have been sold and the price that customers pay for each box. The sales manager wants to evaluate the performance of his sales people. Do an **FI & FO** on the computer report.

2. When a toy company writes TV advertising for its toys, what information is included (**FI**) and what information might be intentionally excluded (**FO**) from the advertising?

FI: _____

_____

_____

_____

_____

_____

_____

_____

FO: _____

_____

_____

_____

_____

_____

_____

_____

Lesson *22*

INFORMATION IN GENERAL BUSINESS

FI & FO PRACTICE: SMALL GROUP ACTIVITIES

In small groups, do an **FI & FO** on the following items.

1. "The way Fred drives, someone is going to get killed. I'm going to report him to the Safety Department."

2. "There will be a meeting on Tuesday at 3:00 p.m. to discuss the new employee counseling program."

3. "The company picnic will be held on Saturday, June 27th. Spouses and children are invited. There will be food, games, and prizes for everyone. Sign up below if you plan to attend."

4. "The Purchasing, Inventory Control, and Transportation Departments will be consolidated into one department to be called the Materials Management Department. The new Materials Manager will be Alice Lee, who is currently the Purchasing Manager."

USING **FI & FO** IN GENERAL BUSINESS

1. What types of information are important within a company?

_____

_____

_____

_____

_____

_____

_____

_____

_____

_____

2. For the following jobs, what information is most important and how is it completely and accurately conveyed?

   a. A worker in a window factory who makes custom-sized and designed windows, one at a time

_____

_____

_____

_____

_____

_____

_____

b. A computer repair technician

_____

_____

_____

_____

_____

_____

_____

_____

c. An accounts payable assistant who writes checks to pay the company's bills

_____

_____

_____

_____

_____

_____

_____

_____

_____

d. A fudge maker in a candy factory

_____

_____

_____

_____

_____

_____

_____

_____

_____

e. A customer service representative who answers an 800 number for a bicycle manufacturer

_____

_____

_____

_____

_____

_____

_____

_____

_____

FI & FO PROJECT 1

Select one of the following items. Use the space provided to do an **FI & FO** on the information provided.

1. The tire manufacturer who has sold you tires for the past three years for the boat trailers your company builds has just announced a twenty-three percent price increase. A tire manufacturer you had used previously is now offering lower prices and wants to regain your business.

2. When you have your annual performance review with your supervisor, you are told that you are a friendly and nice person, but you will not receive a raise this year.

FI: _____

_____

_____

_____

_____

_____

_____

_____

FO: _____

_____

_____

_____

_____

_____

_____

_____

FI & FO PROJECT 2

Select one of the following items. Use the space provided to do an **FI & FO** on the information given.

1. To: The Safety Manager

    These trucks are falling apart. They don't have any power, the brakes are lousy, they are dirty, the air conditioning doesn't work, and the mechanics never fix them when we write up the problems. You need to do something about this before someone gets hurt driving these pieces of junk.

    From: A driver who is a lot better than these trucks

2. Dear Quickspeed Bicycle Manufacturing Company:

    We bought one of your bicycles for our son's birthday. He was really excited until we found there were no nuts and bolts in the box to put the bicycle together. The store that sold it to us didn't have another bike like this and wasn't interested in helping us. We bought the bike on sale and couldn't afford to buy a different one. Tommy cried for two days. What are you going to do about this?

FI: _____

_____

_____

_____

_____

_____

FO: _____

_____

_____

_____

_____

_____

_____

_____

Lesson 23

QUESTIONS

FQ & SQ: FISHING QUESTIONS AND SHOOTING QUESTIONS

FQ = Fishing **Q**uestion
SQ = Shooting **Q**uestion

Asking a question is often the best way of getting information. Sometimes you are just looking for information and do not know what answer you might get. At other times you want a yes or no answer.

Fishing **Q**uestion (**FQ**)

When you go fishing, you put some bait on a hook and throw the hook into the water. You do not know what you might catch. In a fishing question you do not know what the answer is going to be.

> ### EXAMPLE: DOING AN FQ
>
> 1. Who wants to play football?
> 2. What are sausages made of?
> 3. Why do we have examinations every year?

You are fishing for information.

Shooting **Q**uestion (**SQ**)

When you go shooting, you only shoot when you have seen something you want to hit and have aimed at it very carefully. You may hit or you may miss, but you know what you are aiming at. In a shooting question you know what you are aiming at. You use shooting questions to check up on things. The answer is a yes or a no.

> ### EXAMPLE: DOING AN SQ
>
> 1. Were you at school yesterday?
> 2. Do you like math?
> 3. Is that your bicycle?

When asking a question, you should always try to get the greatest amount of information from each question. You should also know what sort of question you want to ask. If you start by doing an **FI & FO**, you will know what questions need to be asked.

112

FQ & SQ PRACTICE: SMALL GROUP ACTIVITIES

Use small group procedures for each of the following items.

1. Which of the following are **fishing questions (FQs)** and which are **shooting questions (SQs)**?

   a. "Do you know who is the heavyweight boxing champion of the world?"
   b. "Who is the heavyweight boxing champion of the world?"
   c. "Who broke the window in the corridor?"
   d. "If you saw someone breaking a window on purpose, would you report that person?"
   e. "What were you doing yesterday evening?"
   f. "Did you watch TV yesterday evening?"
   g. "Would you like a holiday today?"
   h. "What would you do if you had a holiday today?"
   i. "How much money would I earn in that job?"
   j. "Would I get an increase in wages each year?"

2. A teacher is thinking of one of the following things. What questions could you ask to find out which thing it is? Try to find out by asking as few questions as you can.

   potato, rifle, soap, toothpaste, matchstick, football, cow, politician, pig, exam, ambulance, frog, betting, accident, cheese, ring, fog, police, hippopotamus, snail, rose, bee, screw, book, pencil, cornflakes, TV, teeth, bus

3. You are a supervisor interviewing someone for a job. The job is as a driver, a teacher, or a bank clerk. Choose one. What questions would you ask? Think of four **FQs** and four **SQs**.

4. Walking home in the evening after a visit to a friend, an elderly woman is mugged in the street. Someone attacks her and hits her on the head and then steals her handbag which has some money in it. From the woman's description, the police pick up a young man and find that he has almost exactly the same amount of money that has been stolen from the elderly woman. As a police officer you question both the woman and the suspect. What questions would you ask the woman? What questions would you ask the suspect?

DISCUSS THE FQ & SQ PROCESS

1. When do you use an **FQ**? When do you use an **SQ**?

2. If you are not sure of what to do, which type of question should you ask first? Why?

3. Which type of questioning opens up new ideas?

DISCUSS FQ & SQ PRINCIPLES

1. In the process of obtaining the information you really need, you may have to ask several **FQs** and **SQs**. Why?

2. **SQs** are most useful when you want to check on something or verify information. Why?

3. Sometimes you ask an **FQ** even though you think you know the answer. Why?

FQ & SQ PROJECT 1

Select one of the following items. Use the space provided to record your responses.

1. A gang of teenage vandals has been wrecking pay phones and breaking shop windows for no apparent reason. Eventually the vandals are caught. The social worker is trying to find out why they behaved in this way. What questions should be asked?

2. Devise a questionnaire of twelve questions to ask shoppers in order to find out how shopping can be improved.

Questions:_____

_____

_____

_____

_____

_____

_____

_____

_____

_____

_____

_____

_____

_____

_____

FQ & SQ PROJECT 2

Select one of the following items. Use the space provided to record your responses.

1. You are being interviewed for acceptance into a data entry training program at a small, private business school. What **FQs** and **SQs** should you ask?

2. You are being interviewed for a job as an air conditioning technician's assistant. You are told that a urinalysis will be required as a drug screen. What **FQs** and **SQs** should you ask?

FQs:_____

_____

_____

_____

_____

_____

_____

_____

SQs:_____

_____

_____

_____

_____

_____

_____

_____

_____

_____

QUESTIONS IN GENERAL BUSINESS

FQ & SQ PRACTICE: SMALL GROUP ACTIVITIES

In small groups, do an **FQ** or **SQ** as directed in each of the following items.

1. Review the following questions, one at a time. Decide if the question is a fishing question (**FQ**) or a shooting question (**SQ**). Then think of a question *of the other type* relating to the same situation.

   Examples:

   Q: Is the grinder taking too much material off those parts?
   Question Type: **SQ**
   FQ: *What's wrong with those parts?*

   Q: Why are you leaving your work station?
   Question Type: **FQ**
   SQ: *Is it time for a coffee break now?*

   Questions:

   a. Did you join the bowling team?
   b. How do you like the new intercom system?
   c. Where is the copying paper kept?
   d. Will you finish that project on schedule?
   e. Where are the restrooms?
   f. Would you like your coffee with your meal?
   g. When is the delivery expected?
   h. Why are the employees on strike?
   i. Has the mail arrived yet?

2. For each situation, decide whether a fishing question (**FQ**) or a shooting question (**SQ**) is more appropriate. Give an example of a question to be asked.

Example:

You need to know what school work you missed.
Question Type: **FQ**
Question: *What assignments did I miss while I was absent?*

You want to know:

   a. when your homework assignment is due
   b. how to get the drawer back in your desk
   c. if there is a penalty on your late payment
   d. where to return your rental car
   e. why the carpet is wet
   f. if a job applicant is qualified
   g. what happens if you miss a day's work
   h. what happens if you miss a week's work
   i. if you want to do business with a company
   j. if you should buy a particular car
   k. if your customer can accept different delivery dates

3. A key word in many businesses is communication. A vital part of business communication is asking questions. The questions can be directed within or outside the company. For each situation, suggest **FQ**s and **SQ**s that might be asked on a regular basis as part of normal business communications.

   a. A sales representative talking to a customer
   b. A personnel manager talking to an employee calling in sick
   c. A foreman talking to an employee injured on the job
   d. A production worker talking to the foreman
   e. A word processing clerk talking to someone who needs a letter produced
   f. A purchasing agent talking to a supplier
   g. A customer talking to a customer service representative

USING QUESTIONS IN GENERAL BUSINESS

1. How can questions make a company more efficient, more profitable, and a better place to work.

_____

_____

_____

_____

_____

2. How might questions make a person defensive or create resentment? When might they not be well received?

_____

_____

_____

_____

_____

3. How can questions be used in a positive way? How can you avoid communicating the wrong message with questions?

_____

_____

_____

_____

_____

FQ & SQ PROJECT 1

Complete one of the following items. Use the space provided to record your response.

1. You work at a candy company that is considering introducing a new lunchbox treat for children. The product has granola and some vitamin enrichment. It also is sweet and chocolate-covered. Think of a set of questions (**FQ**s and **SQ**s) to ask parents to determine if they would buy this product. Find out what would make the product attractive to them, so this could be stressed in the advertising for the product.

2. The performance of a good, long-time employee has fallen off. Lateness and absenteeism are high, work quality is low. Think of questions (**FQ**s and **SQ**s) to discover the cause of the change in performance.

FQs and **SQ**s: _____

_____

_____

_____

_____

_____

_____

_____

_____

_____

_____

_____

_____

_____

_____

_____

_____

FQ & SQ PROJECT 2

Complete one of the following items in the space provided.

1. You are going to interview for a job with a large company that manufactures major home appliances. The job for which you have applied is a buyer in the purchasing department. Write questions (**FQs** and **SQs**) that you would ask about the company and the job and whether they are right for you.

2. That delivery company is late again! If those parts aren't delivered by noon, we have to shut down the production line! You have just heard this from the production coordinator. Write questions to ask the delivery company to find out why the shipment is late and to determine when it will arrive. Write questions to explore possibilities other than shutting down the production line.

FQs and SQs: _____

_____

_____

_____

_____

_____

_____

_____

_____

_____

_____

_____

_____

Lesson *25*

INFORMATION AND QUESTIONS REVIEW

The purpose of this lesson is to review Information and Question thinking tools. Given a situation or problem, certain information, or facts, are known (**FI**). Other information or facts that you need might not be known (**FO**). Questions can be used to get the information you need to know. Fishing questions (**FQ**) can be used to explore an issue about which you would like more knowledge. **FQ**s help uncover facts or ideas you may need to consider in order to focus on the information you need. Shooting questions (**SQ**s) are specific and are used when you already know enough facts to focus your question on one issue. **SQ**s are questions that can be answered yes or no.

INFORMATION AND QUESTIONS PRACTICE: SMALL GROUP ACTIVITIES

For each of the following items, list what information is known (**FI**) and what information needs to be learned (**FO**) in order to resolve the problem. Then identify questions, **FQ**s to learn more in general and **SQ**s for specific information, that will give you enough facts to propose a solution.

1. You and your fiancee are discussing where you will live after your marriage. Your fiancee says, "I would like to live in the country. I know we were raised and now live in the city, but I have always dreamed of having a horse. Let's look for a place out of town instead of staying in the city." Do an **FI & FO**; then write **FQ**s and **SQ**s to find out how set your fiancee is on this idea.

2. This notice is posted on the bulletin board:

    All employees are required to attend a meeting in the lunchroom at the beginning of each shift on Wednesday. A representative of the United Way will talk about how you can support many local charities through an easy weekly deduction from your paycheck.

    Do an **FI & FO** about this situation. Then write the **FQ**s and **SQ**s you want to ask at the meeting.

INFORMATION AND QUESTIONS PROJECT 1

Use the space provided below to record your responses to one of the following items.

1. You are a supervisor in a clothing department. A stock clerk approaches you: "I've noticed that the boxes of clothing are often one item short. The boxes have one dozen printed on the outside, but contain only eleven shirts or pants. I don't know how many items were ordered because I don't see any paperwork. I get the boxes of clothes that the warehouse clerks stack on a cart. I take the cart into the department and put the clothes on the racks." Do an **FI** and **FO** for this situation. Decide whom you want to question, and write **FQs** and **SQs** to uncover the information you need.

2. You work in the computer department of an electronics store. A data entry clerk has been making mistakes. The records in the computer show that all the mistakes concern how many of each item are in stock. The clerk's errors make the computer say that more items were sold than really were sold. List the **FI** and **FO** for this situation; then write **FQs** and **SQs** to discover the reason for the errors.

_____

_____

_____

_____

_____

_____

_____

_____

_____

_____

_____

_____

_____

INFORMATION AND QUESTIONS PROJECT 2

Use the space provided to record your responses to one of the following items.

1. The company driver took the company van to the garage where it is usually serviced. The people at the garage were supposed to change the oil. When you get the bill for this work, it includes charges for a complete tune-up. Do an **FI & FO** for this situation. Of whom would you like to ask questions? List **FQ**s and **SQ**s you need to ask these people before deciding whether to pay the bill.

2. Your boss left on a business trip and is calling you from an airport halfway across the country: "That new travel agent really did it! The car rental agent says they have no record of a car reserved for me! There is a big convention in town and no one else has a car I can rent. I just hope they got my hotel reservation right. Please call the travel agent, find out what happened, and get them to straighten this out. I'll call you back in twenty minutes." Do an **FI & FO** for this situation. Write any **FQ**s or **SQ**s you need to ask your boss immediately. Write the **FQ**s and **SQ**s you will ask the travel agent to find out what happened and what will be done to correct the situation.

_____

_____

_____

_____

_____

_____

_____

_____

_____

_____

_____

_____

_____

_____

INFORMATION

UNIT 2

Clues (Lessons 26 and 27)
Simplification and Clarification (Lessons 28 and 29)

Lesson 26

CLUES

CS & CC: CLUES SEPARATELY AND CLUES COMBINED

CS = Clues Separately
CC = Clues Combined

A clue is a piece of information that can suggest many things if you make the effort to find out what it might mean. When you put separate clues together you can get even more information.

Clues Separately (CS)

When you examine clues separately, you look at each clue as if with a magnifying glass to extract the maximum amount of information from it. You should try to think of all the possible things it could mean.

EXAMPLE: DOING A CS

A watch dog kept in a house was not heard to bark during the night of a burglary. Examined by itself, this clue might suggest:

1. The dog was asleep.
2. The dog was drugged.
3. The dog knew the thief, since it did not bark at him or her.
4. It was only a fake burglary carried out by the dog's owner for some reason.

Clues Combined (CC)

When you look at combined clues you take clues that have been examined separately and see what happens when you put them together. Some possibilities might be eliminated and others might be strengthened.

EXAMPLE: DOING A CC

In the burglary just mentioned, the following additional clues were found:

1. The jewelry in the house had just been insured.
2. The owners had reported seeing a prowler to the police.
3. The neighbors had often complained in the past about being awakened by the dog barking, but they weren't awakened that night.
4. The burglar had not bothered with some valuable but uninsured silver.

Taken together the clues suggest that the burglary might have been a fake. The owners may have staged it in order to collect money from the insurance company.

The first thing to do is to find the clues. Next consider them separately. Finally, consider them together.

CLUES PRACTICE: SMALL GROUP ACTIVITIES

Use small group procedures for each of the following items.

1. Every morning a man goes to his office in a skyscraper. He gets out of the elevator at the eighteenth floor, says good morning to the receptionist, and then walks up the stairs to his office on the twenty-fourth floor. From these clues can you suggest anything about the man?

2. A murder has been committed and the body is found on a beach near where the primary suspect has a summer cottage. The police raid the suspect's house in the city and find some sand in the cuffs of a pair of trousers. It is January. Examine this clue and list the possible things it could mean.

3. A woman is going abroad. When she gets to the airport, she discovers that she left her passport at home, so she hurries back to her house. She finds that there has been a burglary and theTV is gone. Some money lying on a table has not been touched. Private papers from the desk have been scattered on the floor. The refrigerator door is open but no food has been taken. The bathtub has four inches of warm water in it. The police think it could have been one of the following:

   a. a professional burglar
   b. her brother with whom she had had a quarrel
   c. a TV addict who wanted to watch the world heavyweight fight

   Do a **CC** and consider the combined clues. Which one of these suspects seems most likely? Or is it someone else?

DISCUSS THE CLUES PROCESS

1. Why is it important to examine each clue separately before combining them?

2. How can combining clues help eliminate possible explanations?

3. How can combining clues help suggest possible explanations?

DISCUSS CLUES PRINCIPLES

1. It is important that you do not dismiss a clue before doing a **CC**. Why?

2. In the process of doing a **CS** or **CC** it is important to look carefully to discover as many clues as are available, even if they seem obvious. Why?

3. How do you know when a clue is important?

CLUES PROJECT 1

Use the space provided to respond to one of the following items.

1. A road accident occurs and a motorcyclist is killed. The witnesses tell the following stories:

    Witness A: I was crossing at the crosswalk when I saw the motorcyclist coming right at me. He swerved to avoid me and smashed into the divider.

    Witness B: I saw a bread truck stopping at the crosswalk for someone to cross. The motorcyclist tried to pass the truck and then crashed into the divider.

    Witness C: I heard a crash and ran out of my shop and almost tripped over a tray of bread. I ran to see if I could help the motorcyclist but the truck driver got there first.

    What do you think happened based only on the clue from Witness A? (Do a **CS**.) Now consider the other clues. Who, if anyone, was to blame?

2. A mysterious illness suddenly develops all over the country. It affects only people who have been on vacation recently in sunny places. What does this clue suggest by itself? (Do a **CS**.) Not all the victims have been to the same resorts. Mysteriously, all the patients have red hair. Can you make anything of these clues? What do these clues suggest when considered together? (Do a **CC**.)

CS: _____

_____

_____

_____

_____

_____

CC: _____

_____

_____

_____

_____

CLUES PROJECT 2

Use the space provided to respond to one of the following items.

1. A TV panel is trying to determine the job of the mystery guest, who can answer only yes or no to its questions. From the following answers, can you guess what job he does?

   a. Do you work alone?   Yes
   b. Do you work with paper?   Yes
   c. Do you work in an office?   No
   d. Is your work visible to a lot of people?   Yes
   e. Are you an artist?   No
   f. Do you use a ladder?   Yes

   _____

   _____

2. A sales representative called a week ago to make an appointment to see a good customer, Mr. X. The sales representative is kept waiting in the reception area for half an hour; then Mr. X's secretary comes out to tell the representative that Mr. X will not have time to see her today. This is the first time this has happened. What conclusion does this clue by itself lead you to? (CS) As the sales representative leaves, a truck from one of her competitors pulls up to the customer's unloading area. Do a CC.

CS: _____

   _____

   _____

   _____

   _____

CC: _____

   _____

   _____

   _____

   _____

Lesson 27

CLUES IN GENERAL BUSINESS

CLUES PRACTICE: SMALL GROUP ACTIVITIES

1. In small groups, discuss each of the following items. What do the following separate clues (**CS**) suggest? Remember, consider each one separately.

    a. The last three bicycles produced have the wrong color seats.
    b. The dog in the apartment next door barks every morning at 6:15.
    c. The truck in front of you is weaving within its lane.
    d. Absenteeism is consistently highest on Mondays.
    e. Your best customer placed a trial order with one of your competitors.
    f. The company van is one-and-a-half hours late returning from its morning delivery route.
    g. Sales of beef in your grocery store dropped fifteen percent last year.
    h. In your restaurant, orders for fish items have doubled in the past two years.
    i. One of your best customers has not paid for the last three orders you shipped.

2. Discuss each clue alone. What do they suggest? Then do a **CC**. What do the clues suggest when taken together? What questions do you want to ask in response to the clues?

    a. All four people in the accounting department have resigned and been replaced in the last six months. Reports from the department are now consistently late. The department supervisor, who was promoted to the position only a year ago, hired the new people.
    b. You work for a paint manufacturing company. All the cars in the parking lot have spots on them that will not wash off. The employees are extremely upset. The spots are white. White paint has not been made for two weeks. The city water tower, one-half block north, looks freshly painted.

USING CLUES IN GENERAL BUSINESS

People on the job do not always have all the information they want. Often they must look at the clues (information or facts) that are available and make a decision or reach a conclusion based on the clues.

1. When would a person make an on-the-job decision without having all the information, or clues, possible?

_____

_____

_____

_____

2. What factors, other than clues, does a person use when making a decision or reaching a conclusion?

_____

_____

_____

_____

3. How does a person decide which clues are most important in making a business decision?

_____

_____

_____

_____

4. How does a person know when it is time to stop gathering clues and time to take action based on the clues available?

_____

_____

_____

_____

CLUES PROJECT 1

Use the space provided to respond to one of the following items.

1. A toy company's managers must decide how many toys to produce for the Christmas sales season. They must order the materials and begin production before their customers place an order to buy toys. What clues do they use to decide how many toys to make?

2. A purchasing agent must evaluate a new company from which to buy glue. The agent does not know how the glue will perform, however, until it is actually used on the production line to hold parts together. What clues does the purchasing agent use to decide whether to order glue from the new supplier?

_____

_____

_____

_____

_____

_____

_____

_____

_____

_____

_____

_____

_____

_____

CLUES PROJECT 2

Use the space provided to respond to one of the following items.

1. A personnel manager cannot really know how well a job applicant will work until after the person is hired. What clues does the personnel manager use to decide whether or not to hire someone?

2. A restaurant never really knows how many people will buy food on any day, or exactly what they will order. What clues would people in the restaurant use to decide how much food to order from their suppliers?

_____

_____

_____

_____

_____

_____

_____

_____

_____

_____

_____

_____

_____

_____

Lesson *28*

SIMPLIFICATION AND CLARIFICATION

SF & CF: SIMPLIFICATION AND CLARIFICATION

SF = Simplification
CF = Clarification

Information is often confused and complicated. Before you can understand the information or act on it, you may have to simplify it or clarify it. What is being said? What does it all boil down to?

Simplification (SF) Simplification means making things more simple. Simplification is the opposite of complication. How can you put things more simply?

EXAMPLE: DOING AN SF

A teacher says: "I want Alice, Gloria, Rosa, Natasha, and Lin on this side of the room and Dick, Leroy, Juan, and Kazuo on that side." Since these are the only children in the room, she could have said, more simply: girls on this side, boys on that side.

Clarification (CF) Clarification means making things more clear. Clarification is the opposite of confusion. Are you clear about what is being said?

EXAMPLE: DOING A CF

A boy is about to toss a coin and he says: "Heads I win and tails you lose." What does this really mean? It means: Only I can win in this game.

There is usually a simpler way of putting things. But the most important thing is to be clear.

136

SF & CF PRACTICE: SMALL GROUP ACTIVITIES

Use small group procedures for each of the following items.

1. Each of the following statements can be simplified (SF) and replaced by a single word. What word would you suggest?

    a. He always wants all he can get and then he still wants more.
    b. She dislikes anyone new, anything new, or any new idea.
    c. He keeps moving from one choice to another and back again.
    d. The finish on this car is rough and pieces keep dropping off.
    e. She does not know that other people have feelings — or does not care.

2. The following pairs of statements describe the same thing. In each case, which statement is the clearer?

    a. I do not take sugar in my coffee but I will take milk, cream, or whatever creamer you have. *Or:* I take anything in my coffee except sugar.

    b. In tennis you may hit the ball before or after its first bounce. *Or:* In tennis you may volley the ball, which means hitting it before its first bounce, or you may wait until it has bounced once before you hit it.

    c. A company uses its profits to expand and to reward its investors, thus encouraging further investment. *Or:* Some of a company's profits go to pay those who originally put up the money to get it going. Some of the profits go to expand the company. Both encourage more people to invest in it.

DISCUSS THE **SF & CF** PROCESS

1. Which is more important, to be simple or to be clear? Why?

2. In order to be clear, it is sometimes necessary to make or write each point separately.

3. How do you tell which of two statements is clearer?

DISCUSS **SF & CF** PRINCIPLES

1. If you cannot think of a way to clarify information, you should talk it over with someone else. Why?

2. Simplification and clarification are not always easy; they take deliberate effort. Why is this so?

SF & CF PROJECT 1

Use the space provided to respond to one of the following items.

1. Write out a clear set of instructions explaining how to change a tire on a car.

2. Write out a clear set of instructions explaining how to tie a bow. You may not use a diagram.

_____

_____

_____

_____

_____

_____

_____

_____

_____

_____

_____

_____

_____

_____

_____

_____

_____

SF & CF PROJECT 2

Use the space provided to respond to one of the following items.

1. Someone says: "The function of government is to organize such things as defense, the police, transportation, the education system, and the legal system. The government must raise taxes to enable it to do all this. It must at all times follow the wishes of the people but it can also lead. It must obey the wishes of the majority but also protect the interests of the minority." A good simplification is to say: The government must do all those things needed for the smooth running of society in accordance with the wishes of all the governed. How else could you simplify it?

2. A country has the following immigration rules: "Someone with no family will not be eligible unless he or she has a job to go to. Someone with a job but with more than six dependents will not be eligible. A person with no job to go to will not be eligible unless he or she is a minor and is willing to work as a minor for at least three years." Can these rules be stated more simply?

_____

_____

_____

_____

_____

_____

_____

_____

_____

_____

_____

_____

_____

_____

Lesson *29*

SIMPLIFICATION AND CLARIFICATION IN GENERAL BUSINESS

SF & CF PRACTICE: SMALL GROUP ACTIVITIES

In small groups, discuss each of the following items.

1. In each of the following situations, a decision must be made. What is the decision? What information has little or no bearing on the decision and so can be ignored to simplify the considerations?

    a. "Alex, I think we need a new trucking company. This is the third time that the one we use now has been late. The last time, the driver went fishing with our supplies on his truck; but those fish he gave us were really good. If this keeps happening, we'll have to shut down production or buy supplies locally at much higher prices just to get by. Let me know your decision by 4:00. I'm leaving early to take my son to the dentist."

    b. "Boy, what an opportunity I've got with this new job in purchasing. I want to impress my new boss right away. I want to show I'm better than that clerk who started two months ago. I bet if I cut the cost of everything I buy, that would impress the boss. He looks like a tightwad. I bet he hasn't bought a new suit in two years. Cost cutting might be my avenue to success. I wonder if I should give it a try?"

2. See if you can clarify the following statements:

    a. I was pushing the cart to the loading area when the post came up to hit us and put the television in the repair area.
    b. For rent. Men's room. Reasonable.
    c. For sale. Car with new tires and paint that doesn't smoke. $500.
    d. I had just dropped the letter when the computer stopped and I picked it up and put it in the out basket.

141

USING **SF & CF** IN GENERAL BUSINESS

Often there is a need for clarification and simplification in business. People in different departments use words, terms, and abbreviations that are specific to their type of work and knowledge. Engineers refer to CAD/CAM, computer operators to DOS and CPUs, benefits employees to ESOPs and COBRAs, and transportation people to pigs, pups, and ROROs. They all know what their specific terms mean. They exclude the rest of us, however, by using terms that are not clear to describe areas of their work that may not be simple.

1. How can an employee be certain that a memo will be clear and will be understood by any other employee who reads it?

_____

_____

_____

_____

_____

_____

_____

2. When writing a resume, how can a job applicant in a highly technical area be certain an employee in a personnel department will understand the applicant's accomplishments and capabilities?

_____

_____

_____

_____

_____

_____

_____

3. In each of the following situations, what must be included to make the communication clear? In what way must the communicator be careful to keep the message simple?

a. Vice-president writing a letter to be sent to employees with annual bonuses

_____

_____

_____

b. Supervisor writing an annual review for an employee

_____

_____

_____

c. Quality control coordinator writing a memo to an accountant to justify the need for and cost of new testing equipment

_____

_____

_____

d. Employee writing to the personnel manager about an unfair review by a supervisor

_____

_____

_____

e. Customer writing a bicycle manufacturer about missing parts from a recently purchased bicycle

_____

_____

_____

_____

SF & CF PROJECT 1

Complete one of the following items in the space provided.

1. Write a notice for a company training session. Include everything a person needs to know to make a decision on whether to attend.

2. Write a recipe for 500 gallons of meatball and mushroom spaghetti sauce. Use gallons for liquid ingredients and pounds for dry ingredients. Include all instructions necessary to make the sauce.

_____

_____

_____

_____

_____

_____

_____

_____

_____

_____

_____

_____

_____

_____

_____

_____

SF & CF PROJECT 2

Complete one of the following items in the space provided.

1. Write instructions to enable someone unfamiliar with the area to drive from your home to your job or to the school you attend.

2. Write clear, simple instructions on how to do each of the following:
   (1) staple six sheets of paper together; (2) sharpen a pencil; (3) use a public telephone.

_____

_____

_____

_____

_____

_____

_____

_____

_____

_____

_____

_____

_____

_____

_____

_____

_____

CLUES AND SIMPLIFICATION AND CLARIFICATION REVIEW

The purpose of this lesson is to review clues and simplification and clarification. These tools deal with information. Clues are pieces of information. They may be individual pieces of information or they may be several pieces that, when taken together, give a more complete picture of a situation or problem. Clarification makes information less confusing. It focuses on what is important and it makes things clear. Simplification eliminates complication and presents information in a simple manner.

CS & CC AND SF & CF PRACTICE: SMALL GROUP ACTIVITIES

For each of the following items, examine the clues. In small groups, prepare a clear statement of the problem. Then, simply and clearly, describe an approach to solving the problem.

1. In a juice canning factory, the pipe that supplies liquid sweetener to the fruit-punch mixer is blocked. The best repair technician is on vacation. The pipe isn't cleared out yet. The people who work on the fruit-punch machines are all just standing around. No one knows when the pipe became blocked or how many cans of unsweetened fruit punch were made.

2. The electricity failed at the pet store. The cats can see well in the dark. The fish need the air pumps back on within a half-hour. The dogs howl at the moon. The batteries in the flashlight are worn out. No one in the store knows where the fuse box is. The lights are out in the florist shop next door. In the apartment above the store, the stereo is playing loud rock music.

3. The company truck is one-and-a-half hours late returning from the morning delivery route. The driver has not called. There is a full load for the afternoon delivery route, with many shipments promised to customers. Someone said the driver's girlfriend lives near the morning route. The police do not know of any accident involving the truck. A phone call confirmed that the customer with the last scheduled delivery received the shipment two hours ago. The driver gave two weeks' notice of his resignation last Friday.

CS & CC AND SF & CF PROJECT 1

Select one of the following items. Examine the clues. Using the space provided, write a clear statement of the problem. Then write a clear, simple description of an approach to solving the problem.

1. Jack started with Acme Manufacturing fourteen years ago, sweeping the floors in the shop. He has worked his way up and now runs one of the largest production machines. Six months ago, he lost his oldest son in an auto accident. Rumors are floating about that Jack's marriage is in trouble. He has been late and absent frequently, and his work quality is suffering. You have heard he is late getting home after work almost every night. Jack has enough warning letters in his file to support firing him. His supervisor, said to be a tough, old codger, would like to fire Jack and be done with the problems. Company policy is to work with and help employees with problems. Jack has asked no one for help.

2. Your company makes and sells personal computers to the government. Many computers have been rejected by the government. The serial numbers show that most rejected computers were made on Monday or Friday. Absenteeism is highest on Mondays and Fridays. If quality is not improved, your company may not get additional contracts for more computers. Absenteeism is higher among younger employees. To qualify for a weekly bonus, workers in the production department must produce 750 computers per week.

_____

_____

_____

_____

_____

_____

_____

_____

_____

_____

_____

_____

CC & CS AND SF & CF PROJECT 2

Select one of the following items. Examine the clues. Using the space provided, write a clear statement of the problem. Then write a clear, simple description of an approach to solving the problem.

1. Sales of the coffee makers your company manufactures are down fifteen percent. Total sales of coffee makers in the United States are up seven percent. Sales of coffee makers from the Far East are up seven percent. European manufacturers of coffee makers have seen large sales increases. Your company makes lower cost coffee makers and sells them at low prices. European coffee makers are generally high priced. Gourmet coffee sales are up seventy-three percent. Imported products are less expensive in the United States right now. Your company hired a new sales manager one month ago.

2. In the clothing store where you work, you have just counted all items in the store to see if you have as much merchandise as the computer records show you should have. Many shirts and pants are missing. Your store puts security tags on all shirts and pants. If a security tag is taken past the sensors at the store entrance, an alarm sounds. Security tags are removed when the merchandise is sold, using a special key to unlock the plastic tag. All missing merchandise is the same size.

_____

_____

_____

_____

_____

_____

_____

_____

_____

_____

_____

_____